THE WAY OF TAOISM: FOR BODILY, SPIRITUAL AND ENVIRONMENTAL HEALTH

PHILOSOPHY SERIES: 6

The Way of Taoism: For Bodily, Spiritual and Environmental Health

Rod Giblett

Copyright © 2023 Transnational Press London

All rights reserved. This book or any portion thereof may not be reproduced or used in any manner whatsoever without the express written permission of the publisher except for the use of brief quotations in a book review or scholarly journal.

First Published in 2023 by Transnational Press London in the United Kingdom, 13 Stamford Place, Sale, M33 3BT, UK.

www.tplondon.com

Transnational Press London® and the logo and its affiliated brands are registered trademarks.

Requests for permission to reproduce material from this work should be sent to: sales@tplondon.com

Paperback

ISBN: 978-1-80135-201-7

Digital

ISBN: 978-1-80135-202-4

Cover Design: Nihal Yazgan

Transnational Press London Ltd. is a company registered in England and Wales No. 8771684.

THE WAY OF TAOISM: FOR BODILY, SPIRITUAL AND ENVIRONMENTAL HEALTH

Rod Giblett

TRANSNATIONAL PRESS LONDON

2023

Dedicated to Heath Greville

CONTENTS

About the Author 3
Acknowledgements 5
1. TAOISM IS POLYTHEISTIC 7
2. THE TAOIST BODY 21
3. TAOISM 22
3. TAOIST ECOLOGY 37
4. THE WAY OF WATER 53
5. THE WAY OF TAOIST TAI CHI 69
6. SACRED SUTRAS 85
References 93

ABOUT THE AUTHOR

Rod Giblett is a practitioner of Taoist Tai Chi and the author of *Health Recovery: The Taoist Tai Chi™ Way* (Shepheard Walwyn, 2008), as well as many other books. He is the founder of wetland cultural studies, psychoanalytic ecology and conservation counter-theology. He is Honorary Associate Professor of Environmental Humanities in the School of Communication and Creative Arts, Deakin University, Australia. He is the author of *Middlemarsh* also published by Transnational Press London earlier this year.

ACKNOWLEDGEMENTS

The dedication of this book to Heath Greville is made to her in gratitude and respect as my first teacher of Taoist Tai Chi in 1982 and Gei Pang Lok Hup Ba Fa in 1990.

Grateful acknowledgement is made to the Board of Fung Loy Kok Institute of Taoism for permission to reproduce material from:

Fung Loy Kok Institute of Taoism, *A Path of Dual Cultivation: Teachings of the Fung Loy Kok Institute of Taoism,* Toronto: Fung Loy Kok Institute of Taoism, 2008;

Fung Loy Kok Institute of Taoism, *Goon Yam Gau Foo Ging* [and] *Daai Bei Jau,* Fung Loy Kok Institute of Taoism, trans. Toronto: Fung Loy Kok Institute of Taoism, 2012;

Fung Loy Kok Institute of Taoism, *The Great Learning*[,] *The Heart Sutra of the Perfection of Wisdom* [and] *the Scripture of Clarity and Stillness,* Fung Loy Kok Institute of Taoism, trans. Toronto: Fung Loy Kok Institute of Taoism, 2012; and

Fung Loy Kok Institute of Taoism, *Ten Thousand Buddhas Sutra,* Toronto: Fung Loy Kok Institute of Taoism, 2012.

Grateful acknowledgement is made to Sandra Giblett for permission to reproduce her photo of a statuette of Guan Yin on the cover of *The Way of Taoism*.

1. TAOISM IS POLYTHEISTIC

What is Taoism? I know it is rude to answer a question with another question, but I am going to be rude and ask you, the reader, what do you think it is? Whatever it is, that will be fine for now. As you read this book, your ideas about Taoism or your definition of Taoism might grow or change. Hopefully they will grow or change, otherwise there may not have been much point in your reading this book. Taoism, as Russell Kirkland says, is whatever Taoists say it is. It is not what non-Taoists say it is, nor even what experts on Chinese culture and religion (Sinologists) say it is. You don't have to be a Taoist, or say you are a Taoist, or want to be a Taoist, to read this book. Taoism is not a proselytizing religion, unlike most others. It is not trying to convert you to Taoism, nor am I. You may be a Taoist already without even knowing it, unlike most other religions (if Taoism can be said to be a religion). You cannot be born, or reborn, as a Taoist (unlike some other religions). You tend to grow into it, or back into it. Taoism is a set of teachings with a canon of texts, rather than a philosophy. It is a way of life and being, rather than a way of thinking and doing. It promotes non-action (*wu-wei*), or not doing and letting go.

One thing that can be said with some certainty about Taoism is that it is polytheistic, that is, it believes in many gods and goddesses, not just one (unlike the monotheisms). Polytheism is alive and well in the Fung Loy Kok Institute of Taoism/Taoist Tai Chi Society (hereafter 'FLK' or 'the Society'). This not-for-profit organization is dedicated to bringing the beliefs, practices and benefits of the 'three religions of China' (Buddhism, Confucianism and Taoism) to all communities. One of the aims and objectives of the Society is to bring the riches of Chinese culture to others in cultural exchange. Founded in Canada in 1970 by Master Moy Lin-shin, the Society is active in over 20 countries and is the largest volunteer tai chi organization in the world. The present chapter draws on the publications of the Society, including transcripts of talks by Master Moy and translations of Chinese texts, to present these beliefs and the benefits of practising the Taoist arts of health, including taijiquan and meditation.

The first major book publication of FLK is entitled *A Path of Dual Cultivation: Teachings of the Fung Loy Kok Institute of Taoism* (FLK, 2008). The first sentence of the chapter devoted to an overview of the 'Taoist Deities' introducing the third and final part of the book begins by stating that 'Taoism is polytheistic, which means that there are myriad deities, immortals, lords, spirits and so on in the Taoist pantheon' (FLK, 2008, p.113). No mention is made here of 'religion.' Is Taoism a religion? Of course, it all depends on how you define 'religion.' The 'Preface' to *A Path of Dual Cultivation* addresses this question and gives a direct answer to it by stating that 'in many Eastern traditions, religion is seen more as a school of teaching than as a devotional faith with strict doctrines as is often seen in the West' (FLK, 2008, p.vi). Taoism is a 'school of teaching' that does not exclude other schools of teaching (or 'religions'). Taoism is the way of the way (or Tao). Taoism follows 'the Great Way (the Tao)' (FLK, 2008, p.19). Similarly, Taoist deities are not gods in the sense of being separate beings but are embodiments of virtues or expressions of the body and mind. They are not without but within.

Taoism has 'integrated' Buddhism and Confucianism (pp.vi-vii). It has a pantheon (literally 'all the gods together'), like many other peoples who have a collection of gods, such as ancient Greece and Rome, and other religions, such as Hinduism. The Taoist pantheon is polytheistic. Taoism does not have 'strict doctrines,' but it does have virtues that enshrine values and guide behaviour derived mainly from Buddhism and Confucianism, such as 'the Eight Virtues' of filial piety, sibling harmony, dedication, trustworthiness, propriety, sacrifice, honour and sense of shame (the virtue you should have when you don't have the others) (FLK, 2008, pp.19-29). Taoism is devotional with the study of scriptures and the practice of meditation, and it has faith, hope and love. Compassion is one of its over-riding virtues.

Compassion is embodied in the Buddhist Bodhisattva of

compassion, Guan Yin, who was Master Moy's personally favourite deity. The story goes that he was a sickly child rejected by his mother at birth and brought up by his older sister who later took him to Taoist monks to try to get them to improve or regain his health. He promised Guan Yin that if he regained his health from practising the Taoist arts of health, he would dedicate the rest of his life to bringing these arts to whoever needed them. He did regain his health and he did keep his promise. He spent the rest of his life travelling around the world to lead workshops. Guan Yin's name translates as 'one who hears the sufferings of the world.' She is 'the all-compassionate goddess of mercy' (FLK, 2008, p.117). Guan Yin is usually shown in figurines and paintings holding a vase in which she collects tears from those suffering (see cover photograph of the present book). Sometimes she is depicted holding the vase upright in which she has collected tears; at other times, she is shown tipping the vase from which tears flow out. Guan Yin does both.

In the 'three religion' 'high shrines' with three deities depicted (such as the one shown on the cover of *A Path of Dual Cultivation*), one Buddhist, one Confucian and one Taoist deity are presented. Guan Yin is typically the Buddhist deity, while the Jade Emperor is the Confucian deity and Immortal Lü the Taoist deity. Guan Yin 'represents compassion' (FLK, 2008, p.131). The Jade Emperor is 'the supreme ruler of Heaven' (FLK, 2008, p.123). He represents 'the quality of virtue' (FLK, 2008, p.131) and is 'considered the personification of the virtues of loyalty, devotion and propriety' (FLK, 2008, p.114). Immortal Lü represents wisdom and is often depicted holding a fly whisk with which he brushes away illusion. He is 'the synthesizer of the three philosophical and religious systems of China: Taoism, Buddhism and Confucianism' (FLK, 2008, p.132; see also pp.vi, 11, 125-130).

The first chapter of *A Path of Dual Cultivation* concludes that 'these three great traditions embody teachings of practical living; how we should interact with others, with ourselves, and nature' (FLK, 2008, p.16). Taoist teachings about interactions with nature gave rise to Taoist ecology (see chapter 3 below). Taoist ecology is founded on the Chinese philosophy of five 'elements,' or phases, or 'real forces' (FLK, 2008, p.133). Western culture is founded on the Greek philosophy of four elements (see Giblett, 1996, pp.156-162). The difference between them, and the elements included in and excluded from them, have had profound implications for both cultures' interactions with nature. The Chinese five elements are wood, fire, earth, metal and water. The western four elements are earth, air, fire and water. Chinese philosophy excludes air, perhaps because it is all-pervasive, whereas for western philosophy it represents the endpoint of sublimation. Both cultures value sublimation, though for Taoism sublimation involves transformation of the body back to the original body in the womb, whereas western sublimation involves transformation of the body into the mind and the sublime heights of art and theory. Western philosophy excludes wood and metal, perhaps because they are just raw materials to be extracted and cut up, the stuff of nature, whereas for Chinese philosophy they are repositories and channels for the circulation of energy in the body of the earth.

Qi, or internal energy, is a central concept in this regard. *A Path of Dual Cultivation* defines *qi* as 'the vital energy or life force [...], the energy that pervades all things in the cosmos' (FLK, 2008, p.16, n.1). In Taoist terms, there is no dead or lifeless matter distinct from living matter; all matter is living. There are no non-living beings or things for living beings to exploit as non-living raw materials. *Taijiquan* and other internal Taoist arts of health, such as chanting and meditation, involve the production and circulation of *qi*. *A Path of Dual Cultivation* says that 'in Taoist meditation the *qi* is accumulated, cultivated, transformed and channelled through the body to massage the internal organs [...] Scripture chanting also plays an important role in aligning the body, regulating the breath and massaging the internal organs' (FLK, 2008, pp.7-8). *Taijiquan* complements chanting as the 'emphasis on alignment, [and] strengthening and straightening the spine' in *taijiquan* 'helps promote proper posture and stamina for chanting' (FLK, 2008, p.8).

If any text exemplifies the polytheistic nature of Taoism in general, and of FLK, and the Society in particular, it is the *Ten Thousand Buddhas Sutra* (FLK, 2012c). You can't get much more polytheistic than 10,000 Buddhas! The back-cover blurb of the book states that *Ten Thousand Buddhas Sutra* is 'the principal text of the Three Religions traditions from which Fung Loy Kok developed. As a sacred scripture, it is meant to be chanted together with others in ceremonies that are a form of dual cultivation of body and mind' (FLK, 2012c). Chanting complements other Taoist arts of health, such as *taijiquan* and meditation (FLK, 2008, pp.7, 8 and 108).

Taoist Tai Chi™ *taijiquan* and meditation go hand in hand. Master Moy said that 'if you want your taijiquan to advance you must practise Taoist mediation' (FLK, 2008, p.6). *Taoist Tai Chi*™ *taijiquan* and meditation are complementary arts of health – both physical and mental (see FLK, 2008, p.7). *Taijiquan* is often called 'meditation in motion' and 'cultivating stillness in motion,' whereas mediation involves stillness and 'cultivating motion in stillness.' *A Path of Dual Cultivation* states that 'one of the goals of Taoist meditation is to achieve a state of stillness and centredness by emptying all thoughts from the mind' (FLK, 2008, p.6). Achieving this state involves 'correction of posture' (FLK, 2008, p.7) in the *Taoist Tai Chi*™ internal arts of health and dual cultivation, including *taijiquan* and meditation. *A Path of Dual Cultivation* goes on to state that 'diligent practise of these internal arts helps to align the spine, improve flexibility in the hips and pelvis, and to stretch, tonify and relax the tendons and connective tissue' (FLK, 2008, p.7). When 'the arms, legs and spine are connected [...] movement of the spine propels movement of the arms and legs' (FLK, 2008, p.10). The spine is 'the engine of movement.'

The teachings of FLK, and the Society focus especially on the arts of health, such as *Taoist Tai Chi*™ *taijiquan* and meditation. Taoism is religion in action and contemplation. A brief biography of Master Moy Lin-shin (1931-1998) near the beginning of *A Path of Dual Cultivation* states that 'Master Moy was careful to point out these teachings were more than just a set of movements; they encompassed practical wisdom for living, drawing upon the richness of Chinese culture and the Taoist tradition' (FLK, 2008, p.ix). Conversely, the teachings of the three Chinese schools of Taoism, Buddhism and Confucianism as expressed in FLK and the Society are not just doctrines to study, or even ethical guidelines to follow, but teach a set of movements encompassing embodied practical wisdom and giving health benefits. The title of *A Path of Dual Cultivation* points to the integration of body and mind/spirit in these teachings and to cultivating both by following a path. In them there is no body and mind/spirit dualism as in the modern West (see Giblett, 2008a, chapters 1, 2, and 10).

The path of dual cultivation that FLK and the Society lay out involves 'internal alchemy' defined as 'a process of transformation which changes the body and mind into higher levels of functioning. In the Taoist tradition of internal alchemy, mind and body are not split into separate independent units as in traditional Western thought' (FLK, 2008, p.4). Arguably in traditional Western thought mind and body were not split into separate independent units, but were integrated. They were split in and by modern Western thought first enunciated by the seventeenth-century French philosopher Rene Descartes (Giblett, 2008a, pp.23-24). The late fifteenth/early sixteenth-century Italian artist, anatomist and inventor Leonardo da Vinci was on the cusp of this split (Giblett, 2008a, pp.20-23). In premodern (or traditional) Western thought and culture, body and mind (and land and water) were integrated (Giblett, 2008a, chapters 1and 2). Body and mind, land and water are still integrated in traditional, premodern non-Western thought and culture, such as Australian Aboriginal cultures (Giblett, 2008a, chapter 11; 2009, chapter 1; 2011, chapter 11). In the Taoist tradition of internal alchemy, mind and body are integrated and participate in the tradition of other cultures, as well as counter modern Western dualism and provide an alternative to it.

Modern Western dualism and medicine regard the body as a machine. When the machine breaks down, it is repaired and parts are replaced. In traditional Chinese (Taoist) medicine the body is a system of energy flows; disease is blockage, and treatment is unblocking (see Giblett, 2008a, pp.158-161). The body in Taoist internal alchemy is what *A Path of Dual Cultivation* calls 'the vehicle for the Return to the Tao' (or Source; FLK, 2008 p. 52) in mutuality with nature, whereas in modern Western thought the body is the vehicle and vector for moving into and colonizing the future with the drive for mastery over nature. The modern western body as machine achieves its apotheosis in the Fascist body, the hard, metallic body of rugged surface. It is the vehicle and vector by which modern western culture colonizes the body and the future (see Giblett, 2008a, chapter 6). By contrast, the Taoist body of soft and supple depths and surfaces returns the body and mind to the body of the past as an individual and as a species decolonising both the body and the future. Whereas in the modern West theory and practice are separated, 'the theoretical and the practical aspects of Taoism are skilfully woven together' (FLK, 2008, p.84).

A powerful way in which the polytheistic FLK and the Society guides interactions with nature within and without us, and brings them into greater affinity with nature, is through what is called 'the Five and Eight Animals training.' An entire chapter of *A Path of Dual Cultivation* is devoted to 'the Five Animal Forms' and 'the Eight Animal Appearances' (FLK, 2008, chapter 5). *A Path of Dual Cultivation* explains that 'the Five Animals are referred to as Forms because they represent the more abstract aspects of *taijiquan*, such as bone strengthening, tendon transformation, spinal movement and accumulation of *qi*' (FLK, 2008, p.69). These aspects are more abstract in the sense of being 'more internal in nature' as they 'represent the transformations that occur inside our bodies as a result of our taijiquan training' (p.69). They train 'the internal structure of the body' (p.69) not visible to the naked or untrained eye. 'The Eight Animals are referred to as Appearances because they describe the more concrete aspects of taijiquan such as abdominal relaxation, sitting low [opening the pelvis and sinking the tailbone], balance, shifting weight, and circulation of blood to the extreme parts of the body' (p.69). These aspects are more concrete in the sense of being 'more external in nature' as they 'describe the body postures and appearances that result from practising taijiquan' (p.69). They are 'behavioural appearances' (p.69) visible to the naked and untrained eye. All the animals can be experienced by the diligent practitioner.

The Five Animals of the forms are: tiger, leopard, dragon, snake and crane. The Eight Animals of the appearances are: bull, deer, horse, lion, monkey, ape, elephant, and bear (FLK, 2008, p.69). *A Path of Dual Cultivation* goes on to elaborate in more detail about the Five Animal Forms:

1. 'The tiger represents power and strength. The strength of the tiger is in its bones [...] the centre of gravity of its body is low [...] The training of the tiger is reflected in open hips, enlarged pelvic bone, strength in the legs, and increase of marrow and calcium in the bones' (FLK, 2008, pp.70-71);

2. 'The leopard is an animal whose speed lies in its ability to spring and leap.' To do so, 'the tendons must be very relaxed, flexible and elastic [...] The leopard thus represents tendon training' (FLK, 2008, pp.71-72);

3. 'The dragon is an animal that has a very flexible spinal column. In fact, its entire body is the spinal column.' In the dragon dance, the dragon curls and unwinds, contracts and expands. 'The training of the dragon is the training of elasticity of the spinal column' involving 'movement of every vertebrae' (FLK, 2008, p.72; see also pp.73-74);

4. 'The snake [...] uses the turning of the spine' to move. 'The snake also represents the spinal training.' Together with the expansion and contraction of the dragon, the turning of the snake produces 'spiral motion with upward and downward movement combined with rotation' (FLK, 2008, pp.74-75);

5. 'The crane is an animal with exquisite poise and balance. It is also the symbol of longevity in oriental cultures. In taijiquan, the crane represents the accumulation of *qi* and sense of balance' (FLK, 2008, p.75).

A Path of Dual Cultivation also goes on to elaborate in more detail about the Eight Animal Appearances and how they relate to and complement the Five Animal Forms:

1. 'The bull has a very hard layer of bone on top of its skull and around the crown of its [...] In taijiquan training we are trying to accumulate *qi* on top of the head so that it resembles the thick layer of protection on the bull's head.' This training represents the channelling of *qi* and blood upwards to the top of the head. It is 'most closely related to the training of the dragon' (FLK, 2008, p.76);

2. 'The deer represents the channelling of *qi* and blood [downwards] to the base of the spine [...] The training of the deer is closely related to the training of the dragon and the snake' (FLK, 2008, pp.76-77);

3. 'The horse is an animal capable of running long distances without tiring. The secret of its stamina is its relaxed stomach [...] In taijiquan we are training to relax our stomach and intestines so that the internal organs drop lower in the abdomen. This lowering of the organs ensures that the centre of gravity is low and that the mass is located near the base of the spinal column.' This makes for better alignment of the spine with better anatomical posture of the skeletal structure and more efficient physiology of the organs. 'The training of the horse is [...] closely related to the training of the snake' (FLK, 2008, p.77);

4. 'The elephant walks in a slow, relaxed way, swaying around gently. The walk also has the appearance of mildly bouncing up and down. This relaxed walk is a sign of elastic tendons [...] In taijiquan training we are training to relax our tendons [...] The training of the elephant is most closely related to the training of the leopard since training in both animals involves "changing of the tendons"' (FLK, 2008, pp.77-78), an important concept and process in this training (FLK, 2008, pp.52, 80);

5. 'The ape uses its long arms to swing from tree to tree. It is a

master at shifting weight and using it to propel movement. The ape represents training in weight shifting and arm strength. "Strength" does not refer to tension of muscle but to relaxed muscles and tendons [...] Training of the ape emphasizes coordination between the arms and legs and the rest of the body [...] the limbs must be connected to the spine [...] because the locus of weight-shifting is at the base of the spine [...] The training of the ape is closely related to the training of the leopard' (FLK, 2008, p.78);

6. 'The secret of the monkey's agility lies in its legs [...] The monkey represents strength in the legs [...] The monkey is a very acrobatic animal [...] Acrobatic movements are founded on an enhanced sense of balance, knowing how to balance different parts of the body in stillness and movement to achieve equilibrium. In *taijiquan*, this kind of balance is founded on relaxed tendons, open joints, and low centre. The training of the monkey is related most closely with the training of the leopard' (FLK, 2008, pp.78-79);

7. 'Bears adopt a low posture when they walk, as if they are sunk into their hips. This low centre of gravity gives the bear a stable stance and strength in its legs and abdomen [...] The training of the bear is the training of [...] dropping and springiness in the hips. It requires open hips and a strong pelvic structure. Therefore, the training of the bear is closely related to the training of the tiger' (FLK, 2008, pp.78-79);

8. 'The lion is known for its roar which resonates over long distances. The "lion's roar" in Taoist internal alchemy and taijiquan training refers to the development and training of *qi* [...] The *qi* is channelled from the navel, brought up through the diaphragm and the throat and radiates with breath and speech. Chanting is a way of training the lion [...] In its emphasis on the accumulation and movement of *qi*, the training of the lion is closely related to the training of the crane' (FLK, 2008, p.79).

A Path of Dual Cultivation concludes its account of the animals by stating that 'becoming the animals is a big step in the path of Return' to 'our Source of Being [...] The Tao is our "Source of Being" [...] To return to the Tao, we must reconnect ourselves with the Source' (FLK, 2008, pp.80, 83; see also pp.50-51). Reconnecting with the source ourselves means transforming ourselves – body and mind – into our original nature through the internal alchemy of Taoist training and by following the path of 'dual cultivation of body and mind [which] is unique to Taoism' (FLK, 2008, p.106). Other schools of teaching emphasize cultivation of either body or mind, whereas Taoism integrates them and creates a path of dual cultivation of both working together and complementing each other. *Taijiquan* training can return us to our original nature and enable us to 'regain the health of the Original Body' in which 'our skin and bones and body resemble those of a baby, flexible, supple and spontaneous' (FLK, 2008, pp.10 and 15). Taoist internal alchemy 'starts with transformation of the physical body' (FLK, 2008, p.107), and not with the mind.

The animal forms are the latent, deep structures of internal processes within the body, whereas the animal appearances are manifestations in external actions visible on the surface of the body. These features point to another distinction between the modern Western body and the traditional Taoist body beside mind/body dualism or holism. The modern Western body is a surface of inscription for the law, pain and pleasure to access and train the mind, whereas the traditional Taoist body integrates surface and depth and trains them together. The modern Western body is trained in exercise in which the mind directs the body, whereas the traditional Taoist body is trained in arts of health in which the mind and body are integrated and function together as a whole. The modern Western body participates in sport in which the body is imprisoned in demarcated spaces and in mechanically measured time, whereas the traditional Taoist body plays freely in open, fluid space and flowing, rhythmic time. The modern Western body strives for mastery over itself and the world outside itself, whereas the traditional Taoist body desires mutuality with itself and the world around it. The modern Western body is a machine, whereas the traditional Taoist body is land. The Dragon is not only an animal form in the Taoist arts of health representing the spine in the Taoist body, but also the backbone of the land in the Taoist arts of Feng Shui and in Taoist ecology. *Feng Shui* is the Taoist art of healthy land, mind and body working together. The Taoist 'picture of the internals' of the embryonic human body is also a picture of the body of the earth.[1]

Taoist Tai Chi™ *taijiquan* has a variety of specific and demonstrable benefits. It is described in an old brochure published by the Taoist Tai Society of Australia as:

> a gentle art of health for people of all ages and health conditions. The slow, graceful movements of Taoist Tai Chi increase strength and flexibility and improve balance and circulation. The Taoist style of Tai Chi emphasises stretching and turning in each of the movements in order to gain these and other benefits more effectively.

The brochure goes on to relate that:

> Regular practice of Taoist Tai Chi can bring a wide range of health benefits to the muscular, skeletal and circulatory systems. The flowing movements of Taoist Tai Chi serve as a moving meditation that reduces stress and provides a way to cultivate body and mind. Specific health benefits include:

> 1. toning of muscles, tendons and other soft tissues;
>
> 2. rotation of the joints through a full range of motion;
>
> 3. stretching and alignment of the spine to make it strong and supple;
>
> 4. gentle massage of the internal organs to improve their functioning.

---

[1] All these aspects mentioned in this paragraph receive a systematic, often chapter-by-chapter discussion in Giblett (2008a). See also Giblett (2009, pp.151-152).

From my experience of these benefits in myself, from reading testimonials written by practitioners attesting to them in newsletters published by various branches of the Society and from hearing anecdotes from practitioners about them too, I thought that there was a wealth of material about the benefits of practising the *Taoist Tai Chi*™ internal arts of health that was unknown to the outside world and that could be explored and showcased to it. In 2003 I travelled to North America and conducted interviews with practitioners about the benefits that they had gained from practising the *Taoist Tai Chi*™ internal arts. These interviews resulted in the book, *Health Recovery: The* Taoist Tai Chi™ *Way* (Giblett, 2008b). The book is dedicated to the memory of Master Moy. The frontispiece of the book is a photo of the columbarium at the International Taoist Tai Chi Centre north of Toronto in Canada in which the ashes of Master Moy and others are housed. Further Information about Master Moy, the Fung Loy Kok Institute of Taoism/Taoist Tai Chi Society, classes and other activities is available on its website www.taoist.org. New members are welcome.

2. THE TAOIST BODY

The current obsession with 'the body' in contemporary culture and in cultural studies and sociology has something peculiarly western about it as John Hay (1994, p.43) has argued. Yet this obsession is marked, not only by cultural difference, but also by history and class consciousness to reuse Lukacs' (1971) well-worn phrase. Indeed, as Foucault (1981, p.126) argues, 'one of the primordial forms of class consciousness is the affirmation of the body.' It might not be going too far to claim that 'the body' is, with a high degree of lexical redundancy, a modern, western, bourgeois invention. Such a modern/western/bourgeois invention or affirmation of 'the body' is different from Traditional Chinese Medicine for, as Judith Farquhar (1994, p.78) has insisted, 'whatever it is that doctors of traditional Chinese medicine work on, it cannot properly be called '*the* body.' Rather they work on a system of energy flows between nodal points along passages or channels which experience blockages manifested in 'diseases' or pathologies. In Traditional Chinese Medicine (TCM) and in the consonant theory and practices of Taoism (including *Tai chi* or *taijqiuan*) 'the body' is conceptualised or metaphorised primarily as the earth with a system of energy-flows.

Taoism, *taijiquan* and Traditional Chinese Medicine (TCM) share a similar view of 'the body,' or more precisely, the cosmic body. Indeed, Joseph Needham (1970, p.324), that most eminent of Sinologists, argues that 'ancient Chinese medicine was closely associated with the beliefs of the philosophers who may broadly be termed Taoist.' Needham (1970, p.284) elsewhere argues that 'many of the most important physicians and medical writers in Chinese history were wholly or partly Taoist.' Fulder (1990, pp.13 and 57) concurs that what he calls 'Oriental traditional medicine' had 'a Taoist framework.' Yet the relationship between TCM and Taoism goes beyond mere association or commonality. Kristofer Schipper

(1993, p.124) speculates that 'there are too many areas of overlap between the ancient medical theories and the inner pantheon of Taoism not to see that they are related. It may well be [that] the mystical vision of the body in Taoism. . . has served as a model of reference for Chinese medicine.'

Taoism

Yet the Taoist pantheon is not in any sense made up of 'gods.' Schipper (1993, p.69) maintained that 'the Taoist pantheon' is equivalent to and identical with 'the abstract powers of the inner universe.' These powers are thus not external to humans and to nature but are what Robinet (1993, p.100) calls 'bodily gods' and 'gods of the body.' Schipper (1993, p.123) goes on to argue that 'the true Taoist pantheon exists within us, created by our vital energies… [producing an] ungraspable vision of the eternal forces of nature'… As a consequence for Schipper (1993, pp.2,3) 'the very notion of religion as we define it in the West is an obstacle' in understanding Taoism and Taoism does not constitute a religion in the western sense 'as something setting humanity apart from nature' - quite the contrary as Taoism had as its conservationist motto 'not humanity apart' from nature two millennia before the Friends of the Earth.

Such is the integration of Taoism and nature that 'the Taoist body,' as Schipper aptly calls it of traditional Chinese medicine is conceptualised as 'a landscape with mountains, lakes, woods, and shelters' as Fulder (1990, p.355) puts it. Or more precisely, given that landscape is a surface phenomenon (see Giblett, 2011, chapter 3), the Taoist body is conceptualised as a land with depths and dynamism, not just surfaces and static parts. For the Taoists, 'the human body is the image of a country' (Schipper, 1993, p.100), rather than the country as the image of the human body (and mind) of modernity in which, for example, mountains are figured as the heady heights of the superego and theory and swamps as the grotesque lower bodily stratum and the unconscious (see Giblett, 1996, p.26). Yet the image of the Taoist body as country is, as Schipper (1978, p.357) goes on to argue, 'a correspondence going beyond a simple metaphor.' For

Liu I-ming 'the human body is the country.' An entire 'environmental ethics,' a whole ecological way of life, is implied here as 'the emphasis on *country*,' as Schipper (1993, p.101; 2001, p.92) puts it, 'reflects the interdependence of the human being and his[/her] environment' to the point that the human being is not simply within his or her environment – rather, 'the environment is within us.'

Besides the correspondence between the human body and the country in Taoist thought in which, as Kohn (1992, p.66) puts, it they are 'structured in the same way,' there is an overarching correspondence between this body and the cosmos. Indeed, as Lévi puts it, 'in China the body is perceived as a replica of the universe.' As one Taoist text put it, 'our body is a small universe' (Daoren, 1994 p.49). Later Lévi (1989, pp.105,109) refers to 'the homology between the body of the universe and the human body.' This correspondence is, in turn, part of what Lévi calls 'the equivalence between microcosm and macrocosm,' in which the latter could be conceptualised as country or 'heavens'. The human body for Kohn (1992, p.113) is 'a microcosm of the universe.' Conversely, the universe is what Robinet (1993, pp.13, 133) calls 'a makanthropos,' the human body writ large, and 'each human being is a little universe . . . The human body . . . ends up becoming a kind of terrestrial heaven.'

Whether the relationship between the two cosmoses is one of equivalence as Lévi calls it; or whether 'the unity of human cosmos and heavenly macrocosm' is 'the founding insight of traditional Chinese medicine' as 'we are always told;' or whether there is 'commonality of the outer and inner realms - of nature and human nature' as Kuriyama (1994, pp.31, 33) argues; or whether 'the body and the landscape prove indivisible' as Zito and Barlow (1994, p.13) surmise; or whether there is 'correlative thinking' between body and cosmos, microcosm and macrocosm as Graham (1989, pp.319-325), Bodde (1991, pp.97-103) and Henderson (1984, pp.1-58) argue; or whether there is correspondence between body and landscape as Schipper suggests; or whether the mapping of one body onto another ulitmately deconstructs any sense of metaphorical equivalence or correspondence between the two as a post-structuralist might suggest; the point seems to be that we are dealing with a sense of one body, the (human) body of the earth, not two separate bodies between which some sort of relationship or correspondence exists or could be set up.

There is thus no human being/natural environment dualism in Taoism. Human bodies are co-extensive with and identical to natural environs, principally the bioregion in which one lives and works, which sustains one being, and to which one returns when one dies. *Taijiquan* enacts this holism in which 'the perfect and complete body', as Schipper (1993, p.42) puts it of *hsiu-yang*, the art of cultivating oneself in general, is 'nurtured, its energies strengthened; it thus becomes totally integrated into the natural and cosmic environment.'

In this body of the earth the self is, according to Zito and Barlow (1994, p.11), 'evolving in the relation between the organic microcosm of the body and the social macrocosm of humanity,' and indeed with the organic and inorganic macrocosm of the earth which sustains the human body and humanity. There are on this view, as Angela Zito (1994, p.111) suggests, 'no fixed boundaries between the internal self and the external world'. Nor, for that matter, are there fixed boundaries between internal self and external body as body/selves are internal and external. Self and world are, as Zito further suggests, 'contextualized in a web of interconnection.' *Taijiquan* enacts this holism also as it is 'the embodiment of cosmic patterns to properly attune the self in the world' (Girardot, Miller and Xiaogan, 2001, p.1).

Cultural difference in the understanding of body, self and world can be drawn here markedly as Kleinman (1988, p.11) does:

> For members of [modern] Western societies the body is a discrete entity, a thing, an 'it,' machinelike and objective, separate from thought and emotion. For members of many [pre-modern or] non-Western societies, the body is a open system linking social relation to the self, a vital balance between interrelated elements in a holistic cosmos. . . The body-self is not a secularised private domain of the individual

person but an organic part of a sacred, sociocentric world, a communication involving exchanges with others (including the divine).

And with the 'environment' or 'nature.' The metabolic exchange with 'nature' operates on a continuum from mastery to mutuality, parasitism to symbiosis (see Giblett, 2011), preferably the latter. The human body is, as Hay (1994, p.66; see also 1983) puts it, 'the environment of the viscera' and 'itself within an environment at a higher level.' Moreover, the natural environment is the viscera of the earth and no mere background, context or resource to be related to, lived in or exploited.

In Taoism and Traditional Chinese Medicine there is no Cartesian mind-body dualism. Indeed, Kohn (1992, p.169) argues that 'it is almost a truism nowadays that the Chinese tradition does not radically distinguish body and mind.' Similarly, Fulder (1990, p.267; see also Allan, 1997, p.85) puts it bluntly, if clumsily, that 'the Chinese do not have a distinction of mind/body.' Rather for them traditionally there is what Roger Ames calls a holistic 'psychosomatic process.' Indeed, in the words of the *I Ching*, 'one does not have a body.' Rather, in short, one *is* a body. Or in the words of Chuang Tzu, 'your body is not your own: it is the delegated image of Tao' (cited by Watts, 1953, p.28). Or in the words of Lieh-tzu (1960, p.29), 'your body is not your own possession . . . It is the shape lent to you by heaven and earth,' or as we might say, by nature and culture. For the Taoists, as Ames (1984, pp.44, 48) concludes, 'the body is a 'process' rather than a 'thing,' something 'done' rather than something one 'has',' a performance (exemplified in *taijiquan*), not a product. Although Kaptchuk (1983, p.258) argues that 'the process is all there is,' this process is not random or chaotic but patterned (rather than ordered) as earth, country or landscape in what Hay (1994, p.65) aptly calls 'pattern mapped onto process.' Chinese physicians for Porter (1997, pp.153-154) 'were not interested in the model of the body as a machine. . . there can be no such thing in Chinese medical thought as a Cartesian mind/body dualism.'

Picture of Internals

A rubbing on a stone tablet in the White Cloud Taoist Monastery near Beijing, believed to have been etched in the nineteenth century, illustrates the concept/metaphor of the human body is/as the country (see Needham, 1983, Fig. 1587; Schipper, 1978, p.356). In a commentary on this picture Eva Wong (1987) has shown how it represents a sideways (or sagittal) section of the human torso extending from the rump village at the bottom of the picture and the torso (A) up the spine river of heaven or Milky Way (B); through the internal organs including the cave of the mystery of the kidneys, the 'axle of the river' (G); through the centre and source of energy represented by the cowherd (F), the fair lady weaving (H) who 'connects the positive and negative forces' of yin and yang and the four *taijiquan* symbols (*yin* and *yang* combined) (E); on through the heart as the divine boy stone cutter (I) up through the twelve-storeyed pagoda of the neck (J); across the bridge across the palate over the heavenly pool of the mouth (K); through the celestial jade city behind the optic centre (L); past the moon of the optic centre (M), the blue-eyed barbarian monk (N) and the red sun (O); through the ocular space (S) to Lao Tzu, the meditating man and the putative author of the *Tao Te Ching*, the most-well known of the Taoist texts (P); through the Palace of the Mud Ball of the brain (an apt name!) (Q); across the nine peaks of the top of the spinal column (R) finally reaching the red pearl at the very top (T), the sign of the completion of the circulation of energy in which, as Eva Wong (1987, p.6) puts it, 'the body is internally connected . . . [and] all opposites are united, all fragmentations are undone,' a process which began with the water wheel treaders representing the reversal of the flow of the generative force (C) and which was continued with the tripod of the elixir in whose cauldron the energies are rechannelled (D).

The picture of internals, as it is often called, is thus not a picture of the human body as country as a static structure but as a dynamic process. It is also a journey or story of ever-changing transformation beginning from the generation of energy symbolised by the rump village coccyx and ending with completion and unification. If one word could be said to characterise the Taoist view of the body, as well of 'life, the universe and everything,' it would be change, even from the beginning of life and the body. Schipper (1993, p.116) argues that the 'concept of change (*hua* or *pien-hua*; also: mutation, transformation, and flux), is one of the very basic ideas of Taoism.' In her commentary on this picture Eva Wong (1987, p.1) has suggested that the figure is 'shaped like an embryo and foetus.' Indeed, as Kravitz (1998) pointed out in a public lecture, Frank Netter's (1969, plate 6, p.118) illustration of an embryo at 23 days demonstrates that the figure is a representation of an embryo.

In his caption to the White Cloud Monastery rubbing Needham (1983, p.115) argues that it 'represents the culmination of Taoist anatomy and physiology', though hardly in the modern western sense. The uncanny resemblance between the rubbing and Netter's illustration puts paid to Needham's contention that it 'shows a fanciful poetical rendering of a sagittal section of the head, thorax and abdomen seen from the left-hand side.' Poetical indeed, but hardly fanciful when placed side by side with, or even over, Netter's illustration. Although they do not map on to each other exactly, there is an uncanny correspondence between the two: the Divine Boy Stone-Cutter is the embryonic heart; the Rump Village is the coccyx; the River of Heaven is the spine; the Water Wheel Treaders are the umbilical arteries and veins; the Palace of the Mud Ball is the brain. Even the edges of the field ploughed by the Cowherd where *chi* or energy is produced look like the mouth of the yolk sack in Netter's illustration.

The picture of internals represents the return to the original body, a return back to beginnings, reversing the aging process. The water wheel symbolises the beginning of the reversal of the aging process. The aim of Taoism and *taijiquan* is to return the body (and mind) to the perfection of the pre-natal state, what is called Anterior or Earlier Heaven. The Taoist body is supposedly given birth to by the adult, feminised body. The Taoist's body, 'in this world' as Schipper (1978, p. 363 and 1993, p.129) puts it, is 'the body of a woman, a mother with Child.' Taoism, according to Schipper (1978, p.365), 'at least ideally, identified with the female body' to the point that even 'the Tao's action, its creative power, is ... feminine' (Schipper, 1993, p.4) as 'the female body, the body of the pregnant mother, is the only truly complete body, the only one able to accomplish the transformation, the work of the Tao' (Schipper, 1993, p.129). He goes on to indicate Lao Tzu in particular as exemplifying this body and suggests that he was 'his own mother' (Schipper, 1978, p.371; 1993, p.122). In Taoism, as Lévi (1989, p.106) puts it, 'cosmogenesis merges with embryogenesis' which equates embryo with cosmos, and their births, rather than the western idea of ontogenesis (the birth of the individual) repeating phylogenesis (the birth of the race) which privileges individual and race over embryo and cosmos, and the birth of the former over the conception of the latter. For Taoism pregnancy is, as Schipper (1993, p.117) puts it, 'the paradigm for the creation of the universe,' the 'Round Belly' rather than the phallic orgasm of the 'Big Bang' of modern western physics. Taoists believe that the birth of the cosmos and the conception of the embryo can be repeated or retrieved in the rebirth of the human body through Taoist arts such as *taijiquan*.

For the Taoists there is a gender cross fertilisation in which, as Schipper (1993, p.364) puts it, 'men [and presumably women too] should cultivate a female character,' rather than cultivating a male or masculine character. A female character in Taoist terms is one which values birth and develops a soft and strong body. Arguably the Taoists were not patriarchal but represented an attempt to harmonise or balance gender features and qualities, though they do appropriate birth imagery yet not in a way which denies the exclusive role of women in giving birth unlike in the modern, masculinist birthing metaphors of machines. The figure of Lao Tzu's father 'never really caught on in the Taoist tradition' according to Schipper (1978, pp.364 and 375) and 'the place given to women is especially remarkable and wholly unique for the times.' Indeed, he concludes that 'there is also the possibility that women played a major role in the movement.' In fact, one of the traditional seven Taoist 'masters' was a woman.

Traditional Chinese physicians, according to Fulder (1990, pp.59,60), 'view the body as a purely functional set of processes.' For them, Fulder goes on to explain, 'the body is a dynamic whole, a kind of continuous protoplasm, which could not be chopped into separately working parts.' By contrast modern western medicine, Sivin (1974), p.xiv; my emphasis) argues, 'deals with material structures and tissues which are able to perform certain functions [whereas] Chinese medicine deals with functions to which physically demonstrable organs *happen to be attached*.' In TCM the processes function or perform the organs, rather than the organs performing the functions and processes as in modern western medicine. Organs make up organisms where the same principle applies. For Watts (1970, p.187), 'every organism is a process: thus the organism is not other than its actions. To put it clumsily: it is what it does.' Form follows function. The Taoist body is a performative body, the modern western body is an organised body; the former is a body of doing with things, the latter a body of things which do. Similarly, in *taijiquan*, rather than the player performing the moves, the moves perform the player.

Taijiquan

The Chinese body, as Elvin (1989, p.267) puts it, is 'a peg-doll whose role is to be a carrier of corporeal and/or sartorial attributes.' The limbs and organs are attached to the spine and, in the performance of *taijiquan*, the limbs rotate around the peg of the spine like an old-fashioned peg-doll, the organs are massaged gently and the spine is re-aligned. In Chinese art, and in traditional Chinese culture more generally, as Hay (1994, p.51) puts it, 'there is no image of a body as a whole object, least of all as a solid and well-shaped entity whose shapeliness is supported by the structure of a skeleton and defined in the exteriority of swelling muscle and enclosing flesh.' Muscle was ignored or overlooked.

There is ultimately no hard and fast divide between the surface and depth, outside and inside of the body for Taoism. Depth and inside are considered more important than surface and outside. We are dealing with what Kuriyama (1999, p.166) calls 'a conception of the body structured by the logic of depth' rather than ruled by the logic of surface as in modern western anatomy. In Chinese medicine, Kuriyama (1999, p.166) goes on to argue,

> all changes in the body, physiological as well as pathological, were governed by the logic of depth. . . Shape mattered far less than place: the functional structure of the human body was ordered first and foremost by the polarity opposing the body surface (*biao*) to its inner core (*li*).

Inner core governs body surface. The channels, or meridians, for the flow of energy, as Kaptchuk (1983, p.77) points out, 'connect the interior of the body with the exterior.' There is no hard and fast distinction between the two in TCM and Taoism, nor between mass and flow, surface and depth. The Taoist body is a body of a certain critical mass yet it is also a body of flow, the flow of *ch'i* or energy-matter, or 'matter that incorporates vitality' (Lloyd and Sivin, 2002, p.198; see also p.201), or blood (Kuriyama, 1999, p.229), or oxygen (Kravitz, 1998), through the body, the flow of the movements, and a body of depth, working on tendons, ligaments and organs, relaxing the mind, and harmonising the spirit. Fulder (1990, p.273), too, concludes that 'practices such as *taijiquan* are the primary means to preserve vitality and are the first steps to harmony and self-transcendence.' Yet transcendence in Taoism, as Schipper (1993, pp.40,1) points out, is 'not the result of a spirit separated from matter, an external divine force given to the world, but a spiritualization of *ch'i* , of energy-matter itself.' Self-transcendence is what Robinet (1993, p.95) calls 'cosmicization' of the human body.'

For the Taoists, as Hay (1994, p.66) puts it, 'surfaces were [and are] not impenetrable faces of geometric solids, but palpable interfaces through which the structural values of interiority interacted with the environment,' both the natural and social environments, and with other embodied selves. In the modern western tradition, as Turner (1994, p.14) puts it, 'the surface of the body . . . is the mirror of the self' which splits the body and the self and sets up the possibility of a narcissistic relationship between the self and the body, whereas in the Taoist tradition the self is embodied; the body/self is surface and depth, mass and flow. For the Taoists the body/self is, as Zito (1994, pp.110 and 117) puts it, 'a focussed field with a dense centre that could ideally interpenetrate with other selves' and whose 'shifting edges and surfaces provided the sites for articulation between inner and outer,' not a flat, reflective surface for the contemplation of the self. This self, says Kuriyama (1999, p.245), is 'neither a shining Orphic soul imprisoned in the darkness of matter, nor an immaterial mind set against a material body.' Mind and body are material; the self is embodied.

The Taoist body dances internally and externally with the circulation of (internal) energy and with the (interior and exterior) movements of *taijiquan*. *Taijiquan* involves what Mauss (1992, p.469) calls 'dancing at rest;' it is also what he calls 'a technique of active rest.' In Kristeva's (1992, p.169) novel *The Samurai* the narrator describes *taijiquan* as 'a kind of tortoiselike eurythmics.' One character goes on to elaborate in Maussian terms that in *taijiquan*:

> You dance with your arteries and veins . . . – it's not a matter of arms and legs. Your blood surges forward, draws back, and then the time comes when your body's transformed. It doesn't disappear, but the rhythm of your blood is in harmony with shapes you imagine in space – your body itself is all space, what's inside and outside are brought together and redistributed, magnified almost to infinity, anatomised to infinity.

Taijiquan is an external and internal dance of bodily limbs, organs and fluids choreographed to the imagined shapes and actions of animal movements: stork cools wings, snake creeps down, golden cock stands on one leg, and so on. Every activity of the Taoist body, and not only *taijiquan*, is, in Kohn's (1991, p.229) terms, 'patterned on the rhythm of the world at large.'

The choreography of the body is calligraphy in space. Instead of writing on surfaces, *taijiquan* writes in space. Writing about calligraphy, though it is applicable equally to *taijiquan* and to other 'calligraphies of the body' as de Certeau (1992, p.69) calls them, Schipper (1993, p.42) has suggested that 'it is nature retrieved, spontaneous creation, the secret stolen from the Tao.' Specifically of *taijiquan* Schipper (1993, p.138) argues later that:

> this wonderful method of harmony and well-being is a martial art for the defense of the inner world. The slow supple, dance of *taijiquan*, performed with no apparent effort, is for everybody an excellent initiation into the very essentials of Taoism . . . The daily preparatory exercises [of *taijiquan*] already constitute an entrance into the cosmic rhythm, a way of participating in the spontaneous evolution of nature. As soon as the practitioner enters into this universal movement, [s/]he becomes one with the great mutation of all beings.

Taijiquan entails ultimately what Schipper (1993, p.139) calls 'a 'cosmologization of the individual' rather than a modern western individualisation of the cosmos.

Rather than 'man [*sic*] contain[ing] everything in the cosmos' (Barkan, 1975, pp.1 and 2) as in the western view, for the Taoists the cosmos contains everything in the human body. The Taoists see the individual as the cosmos writ small, as embodied. Rather than 'the human body . . . be[ing] the image of a microcosm,' the macrocosm, or perhaps more precisely the social/natural bioregion, is the image of the human body. Instead of the cosmos being corporeal, for the Taoists the body is cosmic, 'the individual body is the cosmic body' (Ni, 1995, p.40). In the modern western individualisation of the cosmos, as Frank (1990, p.159) argues following Lakoff, 'the body is no longer the metaphor which we employ to understand the reality of the social world. Rather the body is the constitutive image schemata in which we have created that world.' The modern western body is the corporeal cosmos rather than the cosmic body of the Taoists. The reality of the social/natural world for the Taoists is the metaphor to understand the human body and that world is the 'constitutive image schemata' in which they create the human body.

Kohn (1991, p.247) suggests 'the world is me, I am the world' provided the subject 'I' and the ego 'me' are an embodied subject and ego, embodied in the world, and the world in the body. As Watts (1970) puts it, 'the world is your body.'

This is the theory of *taijiquan,* which relates to practice, but what of the practice of *taijiquan* as it relates to health? This is what the theorists say about *taijiquan,* but what about the experience of practitioners? What do they say about it? How do they articulate the benefits they may or may not have gained from doing or performing *taijiquan*? *Taijiquan* is now widely recognised in western, industrialised countries and some of its benefits are readily acknowledged. The slow, graceful movements of *taijiquan* are so well-known that they are occasionally used in television advertisements often just to signify relaxation or a healthy life-style. *Taijiquan* is visually appealing and people who watch it often remark that it looks relaxing. More importantly, the people who do it often say that it feels relaxing, and that it is relaxing too. Yet the practitioners of *taijiquan* often have a lot more to say about its effects on them. The stories of some people who do *Taoist Tai Chi*™ *taijiquan* and who talk about its benefits for them have been gathered together in the book *Health recovery: The* Taoist Tai Chi™ *way* (Giblett, 2008b).

Taijiquan is taught in a number of 'styles' or traditions. *Taoist Tai Chi*™ *taijiquan* is taught by the International Taoist Tai Chi Society. It emphasises the health-restoring and -maintaining aspects of *taijiquan* and other Taoist arts of health and well-being. Health-improvement is one of the aims of the Society. Health, however, is not defined in this book (nor by the Society, I would suggest) in narrow, physical terms, but in broad, holistic terms that include physical, mental, spiritual, emotional, and even environmental health. These arts focus on the physical as the initial means to gain health in the other areas as well. Change the body to change the mind and spirit is a motto of the tradition of Taoism from which Taoist Tai Chi and the Society come.

Health recovery presents Taoism as a bio-spiritual practice

(Girardot, Miller and Xiaogan, 2001, pp.xxxix and xlix), or biospiritual cultivation (Kirkland, 2004, esp. p.43), involving a holistic transformation of mind, body and spirit. Similarly, body, mind and spirit are nurtured within and by the culture and community of the Taoist Tai Chi Society. Yet, as Dr Peter Cook, the former Executive Director of the Taoist Tai Chi Society of Australia, points out, the benefits of this practice are not only experienced by those who call themselves 'Taoists' but are readily available to all who practise this *taijiquan* and are members of the Society or participate in its programs. Health-recovery stories are primarily stories about Taoism and the International Taoist Tai Chi Society, and not just about *taijiquan*. *Health recovery: The* Taoist Tai Chi™ *way*, as conveyed in its title and sub-title, focuses on this and other arts as a way to gain access to, and stimulate interest in, and even inspire participation in, Taoism and the Society.

Kirkland (2004) acknowledges the importance, and validity, of 'what Taoists say Taoism is' (p.8), and not just what dead Taoists say Taoism is, but 'living Taoists' as well. *Health recovery* presents what some people, some of whom may not consider themselves to be Taoists, say Taoism, at least Taoism as expressed in the *Taoist Tai Chi* ™ *taijiquan* and the International Taoist Tai Chi Society, is for them. They are what Kirkland calls a 'Taoist voice' (p.178). Although Kirkland is a sinologist and 'not a Taoist' and his book 'is written by an outsider' (p.7), he has opened up a space in which the likes of *Health recovery* by a Taoist and an insider, but not a sinologist, can be considered a legitimate contribution to the study and understanding of Taoism and as the beginning of a more fruitful and ongoing dialogue between Taoists and sinologists about Taoism.

For too long Taoism has been regarded as a dead scriptural or textual tradition and not as a living oral culture as explored and expressed in *Health recovery*. Just as Kirkland sees the classic texts of Taoism arising out of what he calls 'the collective wisdom of the community itself' (p.58), so too does the contemporary practice of Taoism expressed in the *Taoist Tai Chi* ™ internal arts of health and the International Taoist Tai Chi Society arise from the same source as we have seen in previous chapters with its emphasis on what Kelly Ekman sees as 'the real strength in the wisdom of the group' (cited in Giblett, 2008b, pp. 168, 169).

Kirkland later notes that 'some scholars . . . have been doing excellent fieldwork among Taoists of various descriptions in some regions of China. But . . . Taoist practitioners and communities in other regions have not yet received the same attention' (p.116) — until now as *Health recovery* considers Taoist practitioners and the community of the International Taoist Tai Chi Society in other regions such as Europe, North America and Australia. Kirkland concludes his book by suggesting that 'vestiges of nearly every Taoist idea and practice ever attested in China endure in the minds of someone in East Asia today,' and elsewhere, as *Health recovery* demonstrates.

Kirkland goes on to argue that 'many such people, of course, continue to self-identify as Taoist, both in China and throughout the diaspora' (p.210). The founder of the International Taoist Tai Chi Society, Master Moy Lin-Shin, was a member of the diaspora, as are many of those he taught, whilst others, such as myself, are not members of the Chinese diaspora, but self-identify as Taoist. Even for those members of the International Taoist Tai Chi Society who do not self-identify as Taoist, Taoism has had a significant impact on their lives as *Health Recovery* demonstrates. It is not only possibly the first ethnographic study of a group of *taijiquan* practitioners, but almost certainly the first ethnographic study of a group of western, or non-ethnic-Chinese, Taoists. There is no single, homogeneous Taoism deriving from, and adhering to, a classic sacred text as Kirkland argues (see p.181), but a variety of different Taoism*s* and so a variety of different Taoist bodies.

3. TAOIST ECOLOGY

Taoist ecology is based on the idea of the land, like the body, being an energy circuit. Taoists are concerned with 'the flow of energy in the land' (Wong, 2001, p.122). This idea is exemplified in the ancient Taoist art of *feng shui,* which is concerned, as Skinner (1989, p.xi) puts it, 'with the location of dragon lines [or veins (Wong, 1996, pp.30 and 65-68; see also Wong, 2001, p.136)] of energy in the earth and their interaction with man [*sic*] as part of his subtle environment.' For Cheng (1994, p.123) 'dragon arteries wind through the landscape' or more precisely, as landscape is a surface phenomenon (see Giblett, 2011), they wind through the land, both its surface and depth. In Chinese languages, as Allan (1997, p.56) points out, 'there is no word for landscape as such.' Landscape is a western category that colonises the land conceptually and concretely (see Giblett, 2011) so generally the terms 'the earth' or 'the land' will be used in preference to 'landscape,' and 'Chinese painting' to 'Chinese landscape painting.'

In Chinese terms energy or 'life-force' is *ch'i* which 'flows through the earth like an underground stream' (Skinner, 1989, p.1). *Ch'i* also flows through the earth like energy through the body. Thus for Skinner (1989, p.1) 'a parallel can be drawn with the flow of *ch'i* through the acupuncture meridians through the body.' Conversely, a parallel can be drawn with the flow of energy through the earth. *Feng-shui* is a kind of ecological *tai c'hi* as Wong (1996, p.46) defines it as 'the art of seeing the pattern of movement and stillness in the land' just as *tai c'hi* is the art of performing movement with, and cultivating stillness in, the body (as we saw in the previous chapter). Acupuncture, *feng-shui* and *tai c'hi* are Taoist arts of health, longevity and well-being for the body and the earth, for the body of the earth.

And for the health of both. Richard Jefferies (1885/2001, p.92), the late Victorian nature writer, related that in order 'to discover the minute differences, which make one locality healthy and home happy, and the next adjoining unhealthy, the Chinese invented the science of *Feng Shui*, spying about with cabalistic mystery, casting the horoscope of an acre.' *Feng Shui* is Chinese geomancy (Skinner, 1982).

The body and the earth form the body of the earth, what Rossbach (1984, p.8) calls 'a sacred metabolic system' of energy flows in living beings rather than the secular metabolic exchange of dead matter in industrial capitalism (as we saw in a previous chapter). Whereas the former is enacted in the cultivation and circulation of energy in the living body of the earth, the latter culminates in the production of the commodity and in the exchange of dead matter and labour for money, and of money for dead matter. And whereas the latter gives rise to nature as 'man's [*sic*] inorganic body' from which 'he' is alienated and on which 'he' works in the production of commodities, the former is intimately related to nature as humans' body with which humans are united and (with) which humans work (see Giblett 2011).

If land is an energy circuit, and if lands and humans are interconnected then the human being, and body, is an energy circuit too. *Ch'i* or matter/energy is central to a Taoist environmental ethos (rather than ethics (see Ames, 1986, p.341)) and to a Taoist view of the body and of the earth, the body of the earth. *Ch'i* for Wei-Ming (1989, p.76) is 'the blood and breath of the vital force that underlies all beings.' The *Guanzi (Chuang Tzu)* calls water 'the blood and breath of the earth' (cited by Kurijama, 1999, p.50). *Ch'i/qi*, or vitality as Allan (1997, p.60) as translates it, is 'closely associated with breath – and mist, the breath of the earth. . . and in later theory it is said to be that which everything is made of.' For Cheng (1994, p.117) 'the vital breaths simultaneously animate both the being of the universe and the being of man [*sic*].' One breath, two beings: human being and the being of the universe are distinct and not merged into one whole but breathe the same breath.

Ch'i/qi contrasts with some major western concepts, such as matter. It occupies according to Graham (cited by Allan, 1997 p.88):

the place in Chinese cosmology occupied by matter in ours.

The basic metaphor behind the word matter is of timber (Latin *materia*), inert and cut up and to be assembled by a carpenter; *qi*, on the other hand, is in the first place breath, alternating between motion and stillness.

In Chinese cosmology the body and the earth are both made of the same living, vital breath (see Cheng, 1986, pp.362-363). In western cosmology the body and the earth are both made of the same inert and desiccated matter. Matter is dry whereas breath is wet.

Blood is wet too, and so *ch'i/qi* is linked to it, and both are linked to water which is the life-blood of the earth and the major component of the human body. Water in the *Guanzi* is 'the blood and *qi*-breath of the earth' (cited by Allan, 1997, p.123). Conversely, *qi* is the water and breath of the body. Consequently for Wei-Ming (1989, p.78) 'we are consanguineous with nature.' We share the same blood, and breath, of *ch'i* as nature. The same *ch'i* is pumped and flows through our veins and arteries, airways and lungs, as flows through the rest of nature. Interestingly, in the four element (and humour) theory of western philosophy air and the gaseous are associated with the wet and sanguineous (see Giblett, 1996, pp.156-160).

The *ch'i* in the plural for Graham (1989, p.325) are 'the energetic fluids in the atmosphere and inside the body.' They are not a singular substance and they are not confined to single, self-contained entities but run through the body and the earth. The *Chuang-tzu* states that 'running through the whole world there is nothing but the one *ch'i*' (quoted by Graham 1989, p.328). *Ch'i* for Sullivan (1962, p.7) is 'the breath of the universe.' The idea of breath for Cheng (1994, p.118) 'is at the core of Chinese cosmology,' including traditional medicine. Indeed, medicine is a part of cosmology as Cheng goes on to argue that 'every living thing is primarily conceived not as a mere substance but as a condensation of the different types of breaths that regulate its vital functioning.'

In early Chinese thought the waterwheel depicted in the Picture of Internals interconnects the two bodies of the human body and the body of the earth. The waterwheel, according to Wong (2000, p.16), is '*both* the Microcosmic and the Macrocosmic Circulations and it is the 'vehicle' that moves energy in the body.' In the microcosmic terms of the body, the waterwheel for Chung is 'movement in the body.' In the macrocosmic terms of the earth, for him the waterwheel 'moves through water' (Wong, 2000, p.95). It is moved by and through water and thereby generates energy. In Chinese cosmology and medicine the kidneys are associated with water (Wong, 2000, pp. 61, 69 and 119). The kidneys are the place or organ where *ch'i* is generated and stored (Wong, 2000, pp. 96-7 and 102).

Correspondingly, wetlands as the 'kidneys' of the earth are the site or 'organ' where the life-giving vitality of water is generated and stored. Both are places of the life-giving flow of water, not of foul stagnancy. In Chinese cosmology and medicine the liver is associated with wood and 'in wood the sap must flow' (Hammer, 1990, p.57) or else the tree will die just as in the body of the earth water must flow or the earth will die. The liver energies, Hammer (1990, p.64) goes on to relate, 'play a major part in the movement and circulation of *ch'i* and the prevention of stagnation.' Although wetlands have been regarded as stagnant, they are dynamic systems often of subsurface water flows. They are vital for life. Like wetlands, the kidneys for Chung (Wong, 2000, p.121) are 'the root and foundation of life.' The human body and the body of the earth are connected in and by the life-giving movement of energy. Cultivating the body, spirit and environment is a path of triple cultivation.

The traditional Chinese, or Taoist, cosmology has profound implications for Chinese painting. Even perspective, that linchpin of Renaissance and modern painting, is different in the Chinese tradition. Chinese perspective, Cheng (1994, p.91) argues, is 'different form linear [single point] perspective, which presumes a privileged vantage point and a point of convergence. . . It is a double perspective' that for Cheng (1994, p.96) 'finally transforms the relationship of subject and object' to the point where 'the outside becomes the inner landscape of the subject.' Land becomes body, becomes the land of the body, as the land becomes body. There is no separation between body and land, though they are not merged in an oceanic Romantic feeling of oneness.

A Chinese artist for Cheng (1994, p.2; see also p.62) 'aspires to the ideal of realizing a living microcosm in which it is possible for the macrocosm to function.' The macrocosm of the universe functions in and through the microcosm of the body. For instance, the T'ang (618-907 CE) style of Chinese painting for Cheng (1994, p.3) 'aims primarily at catching the tonalities of a landscape in their infinite nuances, at capturing the secret vibrations of objects bathed in the invisible breaths which animate the universe.' One such set of 'objects' is mountains. For Sullivan (1962, p.1):

> to the Chinese all mountains are sacred . . . because, since remote times, the Chinese have held that the cosmic forces, the energy, harmony, and ceaseless renewal of the universe, are in some way made manifest in them. In popular belief the mountains is the body of the cosmic being, the rocks its bones, the water the blood that gushes through its veins, the trees and grasses its hair, the clouds and the mists the vapour of its breath - the cosmic breath (*ch'I*), of cloud-breath (*yün-ch'i*), which is the visible manifestation of the very essence of life.

Chinese 'aesthetics' (though aesthetics is arguably a modern western concept like the body and landscape) for Cheng (1994, p.viii):

> being based on an organicist conception of the universe, proposed an art that would strive to re-create a total microcosm, in which the unifying action of breath-spirit plays the leading role, and which emptiness, far from being synonymous with vagueness of arbitrariness, is the inner locus where the network of *vital breaths* [*ch'i*, p.100] is established.

Later Cheng (1994, p.35) relates emptiness to *tai chi*. *T'ai chi* is a succession of empty and full movements. It begins with 'empty steps' in which the foot is placed without transferring weight, then weight is poured into it to become full, and then emptied again in taking the next step forward or back, or in moving the weight back or forwards. This succession begins in the feet and then spreads to other parts of the body. Parts of the body, and the body as a whole, are not passive and active with one active part acting on another passive part. Empty and full are not passive and active, both as features of land and body.

Emptiness in the Chinese perspective for Cheng (1994, p.36) is not:

> as one might suppose, something vague or non-existent. It is dynamic and active. Linked with the idea of the vital breaths and with the principle of the alternation of *yin* and *yang*, it is the pre-eminent site of transformation, the place where *fullness* can attain its full measure. Emptiness introduces discontinuity and reversibility into a given system and thus permits the elements composing the system to transcend rigid opposition and one-sided development . . . [and] create a relationship of open reciprocity between the subject and the objective world, thus *transforming living time into living space*' (my emphasis).

This transformation is quite unlike the modern western transformation of infinite temporality into infinite spatiality by sublimation and the annihilation of space by time in sublime communication technologies (see Giblett, 2008c).

Emptiness for Cheng (1994, p.58) 'fosters interaction, even transmutation, between heaven and earth, and thereby, between space and time' again unlike the modern western sublimation and transcendence of earth into the heavens, and the overcoming of space by time. Chinese painting for Cheng (1994, p.97) moves 'toward a symbiosis of time and space, and through that, toward a symbiosis of man [*sic*] and the universe.' Unlike the pleasing prospects of the gentleman's park estate stretching out in front of one in space and time colonising and enclosing the land and the future, Chinese painting marries time and space in mutual sustainability so that the future is not colonised and enclosed by the past and the present but remains open to new possibilities, new opportunities, to change and growth.

This difference is found in the presentation (or lack of it) of human figures in painting. Unlike in the west with its landscape paintings of the gentleman and his wife situated as owners of the land as private property as in Gainsbrough's *Mr and Mrs Andrews,* or of the lone Romantic hero positioned in sublime isolation against the mountainous landscape or cloudscape, or both as in Casper David Friedrich's *Traveller looking over a sea of fog,* or the countless landscape paintings devoid of human figures which may show traces of human labour but which naturalise it, in China 'landscape painting' for Cheng (1994, p.134) was 'not a naturalist art in which man's [*sic*] presence was reduced or from which he was absent altogether; nor was it an animist art through which man sought to anthropomorphize the external forms landscape.' Human's presence and activity are acknowledged and represented.

Culture and nature are thus not set up in a binary opposition but are complementary just like *yin* and *yang* which for C.-y. Cheng (1986, p.364) exemplify and enact 'the principle of opposite complementarity' unlike the binary oppositions of western mathematics and modern social sciences, and of culture and nature. Nature, as F. Cheng (1994, p.133) puts it, 'is not envisaged as a mere external framework or a term of comparison; it holds out to man [*sic*] a fraternal mirror permitting him to discover and to go beyond himself' by going inside himself and nature rather than being a misogynist screen onto which he projects his phantasies (fears and desire) or a narcissistic mirror in which he contemplates his own egotistic reflection writ large (see Giblett, 2011). Land is troped and lived as living, land as body, body as land, not land as dead, not landscape as body (as in modern western culture (see Giblett, 1996, Figure 1)).

Both the Taoists and the west share a common concern with the sublime and sublimation but how this is conceptualised and enacted is quite different. The Taoist sublime involves the transformation of both body and mind, not just transformation of body into mind as in the western sublime. The Chinese, for Kohn (1992, p.11), 'concentrate on the transformation of body and mind.' The Taoist sublime involves the transformation of body and mind as a whole and not the transformation of body into mind as separate dualistic entities. For Po-tuan (1987, p.29) (c.983-1082 CE) 'those who understand both essence and life, who have bodies outside their bodies (see also p.53), who are both physically and mentally sublimated and who join the Tao and merge with reality are celestial immortals.' Po-tuan (1987, pp.141, 146 and 189) later argues that 'body and mind are both sublimated' and that 'body and mind [are both] forgotten, physically and spiritually sublimated, merging with the Tao in reality.' Sublimation of body and mind (holistic) into healthy mind-body occurs, not sublimation of body into mind (dualistic).

In traditional Chinese philosophy the body and the earth, the body of the earth, is made up of five 'elements' or forces related to virtues (good deeds) and organs (I-Ming, 1988, p.75; Po-Tuan, 1986, p.65 and 1987, pp.30, 48; compare the European philosophy of the four elements related to humours (states of mind and body); see Giblett, 1996, pp.156-162):

ELEMENTS OR 'REAL FORCES'	Metal	Wood	Water	Fire	Earth
ORGAN, FUNCTION	Lungs	Liver	Kidneys and genitals	Heart	Spleen
VIRTUE, 'PRIMALLY INHERENT REALITIES'	Justice	Humaneness (benevolence)	Intelligence (wisdom)	Courtesy	Truthfulness
EMOTIONS, 'TEMPORALLY ACQUIRED ARTIFICIALITIES' OR 'REBELS'	Anger	JOY	Sorrow (sadness)	Delight (happiness)	Desire

REPRESENT, BASES	Sense	Essence	Vitality	Spirit	Energy
THINGS	Wandering higher soul	Ghostlike lower soul	Earthly vitality	Discriminating Mind	Errant intent

Why is there no force or phase of air in Chinese cosmology? Because air, like *ch'i/qi*, is all-pervasive and invisible unlike earth, fire, water, metal and wood. Air (or gas) is the end-point of western sublimation.

What Cheng (1986, p.365) calls 'the Chinese notion of the natural environment' (see pp.352-353) is 'totalistic, phenomenalistic, and organismic.' He goes on to argue that (1986, p.367) 'man [*sic*] is part of the environment; the environment is part of man, and they are both part of the same whole.' Cheng (1994, p.139) maintains that 'we are in the presence of a unitary conception of the universe, which nevertheless implies the inner, dialectical relationship of man [*sic*] and nature.' Both Chinese and western cultures share a sense of dialectical exchange between humans and nature, but how this is conceptualised and enacted is quite different. Cheng (1986, p.353) argues that:

> whereas the West focuses on the external relation of man [*sic*] to his surroundings based upon a qualitative separation and confrontation between the human and non-human worlds, the Chinese focus on the internal relation of man [*sic*] to his surroundings based upon an integrative interdependence and a harmony between man [*sic*] and the world.

Or perhaps in more contemporary terms that smack less of Romanticist notions of harmony, ecological sustainability in bio- and psycho-symbiosis (see Giblett, 2011). The idea of the land being an energy circuit by no means ended with the Taoists. It can be found in what I call the soil conservation classics of the 1930s and 40s. Aldo Leopold, the father of modern American conservation, Albert Howard, the father of organic farming, and Elyne Mitchell, the mother of Australian conservation, amongst others, all acknowledged and argued for healthy lands as the basis for healthy bodies. Leopold went one step further and argued for a holistic concept of land and society as a single organism. In 1942 he asked rhetorically 'who is the land?' and replied 'we are' (Leopold, 1999, p.4). This concept of people and place as one has a much longer genealogy going back to the ancient Taoists whose art of *feng-shui* sees the body and the earth as a single being. This concept of people and place as one is also found amongst Australian indigenous peoples for whom land is body, and body is land (see Giblett 2008a, chapter 11; 2011, chapter 12,

Sir Albert Howard (1947/1972, p.12) summed up his life's work in a number of laws, including the law that 'the health of soil, plant, animal and man [*sic*] is one connected chain.' He goes on later to equate health of the soil with fertility and to connect it with human health. In chapter 10 of *The Soil and Health* entitled 'Soil Fertility and Human Health' Howard. (1947/1972, p.173) asks the question: 'what of the effect of a fertile soil on human health?' Conversely, what of the effect of an infertile, degraded, salinity-affected soil on human health, including mental health? Healthy soil is connected with human health, and conversely human health with soil fertility as Howard (1947/1972, p.175) recognised what he called 'the connection between soil fertility and health.' The chain connecting them and plants and other animals was interlinked and intertwining.

Yet all the links in the chain do not operate equally, or have equal importance. Plants, humans and other animals growing above the ground all depend on the soil below ground for sustenance and survival, and on soil fertility for health. For Howard (1940, p.39; see also p.165) 'the maintenance of soil fertility is the real basis of health [including public health (p.176)] and of resistance to disease.' In referring to human health Howard is thus not just including individual human health but also social public health. What is health?

Howard redefines health in terms of the relationship between humans and their environment without being more specific. For Howard (1940, p.180) 'medical investigations should be deflected from the sterile desert of disease to the study of health – to mankind in relation to his [sic] environment.'

Similarly ecological investigations should be deflected from diagnosing and trying to cure the diseased state of the environment to the study and promotion of health – to the health of the environment in relation to the health of humankind. If medicine should be the study and promotion of health (rather the diagnosis, treatment and curing of disease), and if health should embrace humans in their relationship to their environment, then ecology should be deflected from the sterile diseases of desertification and salinisation to the study and development of health – to the environment in relation to humankind. Ecology should be the study and promotion of health as well as the prevention and curing of disease. If human health and soil fertility are connected, then diseases of humans and the soil are connected.

Writing in the aftermath of the Great Depression of the 1930s and its dust bowl in the United States, Howard (1940, p.139) regarded soil erosion as a disease of the soil. In fact, it is 'a man-made disease' (p.140). For Jock Pick (1944, p.53) too writing in the 1940s about Australia's 'dying heart' as he called it, soil erosion is 'the canker which is, slowly but surely, eating out the heart of the continent.' For Pick 'the centre of the continent' is 'the dying heart' (p.67). Soil erosion for Pick is 'an enemy within the gates . . . a destroyer more deadly than all the Hitlers of history' (p.91). Soil erosion is a terrorist whose genocide is not confined to humans. It infiltrates the citadel of the nation-state whose boundaries are just as permeable and circumnavigable as the Maginot Line was for Hitler's 'Blitzkreig' of tanks and bombers.

Instead of regarding the nation as a castle it may be wiser ecologically to regard it as a body. The body politic was a metaphor for the relationship between king and country in two senses of subjects and lands. In post-monarchical, modern 'democratic' societies the country is no longer an extension of the king's body. The commons are enclosed into private ownership and public lands are managed by the state. Yet reviving a sense of the body politic/ecologic may help to revive and reconfigure the interrelationship between humans and the environment. The Chinese Taoists figured the body as land as we have seen in the previous chapter and the land as body as we have seen in the present chapter.

As soil and soil fertility are the first links in the chain connecting the health of soil, plant, humans and other animals, food is the vital link between humans and the soil and its health. In chapter 12 of *An Agricultural Testament* entitled 'Soil Fertility and National Health' Howard (1940, p.171) considers 'the possible connection between the produce of a fertile soil and the health of the people who have to consume it.' Food is the linchpin of this possible connection. Howard (1940, p.174) concludes that 'the greatest single factor in the production of good health is the right kind of food and the greatest single factor in the production of bad health is the wrong kind of food'.

Elyne Mitchell, the writer of the 'Silver Brumby' stories for children, subscribed to and elaborated similar views to Howard in the 1940s. Unsurprisingly her 1946 book *Soil and Civilization* refers to Howard, in the bibliography. In it she promotes 'land sense' rather than simply a sense of place (Mitchell, 1946, p.33). Like Howard, she refers to 'the health of the land' (Mitchell, 1946, p.83). Unlike Howard she goes much further in articulating the connection between humans and the land. She insists on 'the integral unity of man [*sic*] and the earth' (Mitchell, 1946, p.4) to the point that the land for her is not separate but 'part of the entity, body and soul, that is each individual' (Mitchell, 1946, p.5). The earth is not a thing apart from humans. Rather for her 'the earth is part of themselves' (Mitchell, 1946, p.27). Humans are elemental creatures as for Mitchell (1946, p.74) 'Man [*sic*] on this earth has a body made up of the earth, the water, the air.' And of fire, the energy of the sun that powers all life on this planet.

Yet despite this unity and sense of a single entity made of earthly elements, there is disunity between the two so she insists on 'the absolute necessity of fusion between man [*sic*] and the land' (Mitchell, 1946, p.11). Her idea of fusion promotes symbiosis *with* the land rather than 'living parasitically' (Mitchell, 1946, p.48) *off* the land as white Australians do which Mitchell (1946, p.67) later critiqued when she states 'how heedless Australians are of the land that gives them life.' Symbiosis entails mutual benefit between living partners rather than one partner taking parasitically to the point of killing the other (see Giblett, 2011). To rectify this state of affairs, this state of the environment and of human health, Mitchell (1946, p.127) argues that 'a creative civilization requires a sacramental attitude towards nature.' Rather than a capitalist and sanctuarist attitude towards nature that exploits nature and only conserves it in reserves, Mitchell is a proponent of mutuality and sacrality that promotes symbiosis and sustainability (see Giblett, 2011).

For both partners of humans and the earth to go on living together, both need to go on living. In the case of the relationship between humans and the soil, the latter needs to be regarded as living just as much as the former. Mitchell (1946, p.53) refers to 'living soil,' to 'living earth' and insists that 'every country must have living soil' (Mitchell, 1946, p.132). Why? Because for her 'the economy of each nation must. . . be based on the health of the soil – not on the minerals of the deep earth or the profit of trade' (Mitchell, 1946, p.128). Economy is, or should be, a matter of the surface of the land and its production, not of the depths. Why? Because working the surface of the earth is sustainable and renewable whereas working the depths is not, such as in the extraction of oil, gas and water. By working the depths of the land and extracting oil, water and gas tens of thousands of years old the heritage of the land, what the land has bequeathed us, cannot be passed on to future generations.

Land has, or is, a cultural heritage. Cultural heritage is not just built, artifactual or archival heritage but also the land that sustains cultures. Mitchell (1946, p.107) refers to 'the cultural heritage of a land.' Soil is a matter of cultural heritage, not just of natural heritage placed on the other side of a culture/nature opposition: the cultural heritage of a nation is *the* land. Heritage is what we have inherited from the past and what we pass on to the future in a better or worse state than we inherited it. For Mitchell (1946, p.32) 'the soil, in a large measure, is the people and their future.' Soil is past, present and future. Ecology is a matter of time just as much as it is a matter of space. It is a matter of conserving and rehabilitating the cultural heritage of the soil (not just of buildings, artifacts and archives, nor just of natural heritage) given to us by the past for the future.

For Mitchell (1946, p.64) 'water and soil form the matrix of all culture.' For her, 'the soil is properly regarded as the matrix of our being' (Mitchell, 1946, p.88); 'the soil is the matrix of our lives' (Mitchell, 1946, p.101) and 'the soil [is] the acknowledged matrix of ourselves and our art' (Mitchell, 1946, p.104). Yet land and soil are not synonymous – soil is the Earth Mother or Mother Nature of a benign and malign agriculture whereas land is the Great Goddess, the Great Mother of the earth. The matrix is the grid of farm and town, drains and roads, railway, power and telephone lines, inscribed in soil on the surface of the earth that exploits and depletes the depths of the earth. The matrix is the surface of the land, the landscape (and the portrait) set up vertically against the land rather than the body of the earth in its volume, vitality and horizontality contiguous and continuous with the land.

Writing also in the 1940s, Aldo Leopold also distinguished between land and soil. Land for Leopold (1949, p.216) 'is not merely soil; it is a fountain of energy flowing through a circuit of soils, plants, and animals.' Leopold provided the missing fourth element of fire or energy to Mitchell's three other passive elements: earth, air and water. Leopold (1949, p.218) regards 'land as an energy circuit.' Mitchell promoted 'land sense' as we have seen whereas Leopold advocated a land ethic. For Leopold (1949, p.221) 'a land ethic . . . reflects the existence of an ecological conscience, and this in turn reflects a conviction of individual responsibility for the health of the land.

Health is the capacity of the land for self-renewal. Conservation is our effort to understand and preserve this capacity.' Land is economic base, spatial location and temporal trajectory upon which 'society' depends.

Yet modern society for Leopold (1935, p.217) has:

> developed an unstable adjustment to its environment, from which both must eventually suffer damage or even ruin. Regarding society and land collectively as an organism, that organism has suddenly developed pathological symptoms, i.e. self-accelerating rather than self-compensating departures from normal functioning.

Land health is the normal functioning of the land and society organism. Leopold (1999, pp.22 and 219) defined land-health as 'the capacity for self-renewal in the biota.' By implication, land sickness is the destruction wreaked upon the biota so that it is incapable of self-renewal. As there is physical and mental health, and physical land health, so there is mental land health, and illness, in the psychogeopathology of self-accelerating departures from normal functioning, such as in mining (see Giblett, 2011, chapter 9).

4. THE WAY OF WATER

Water exemplifies the soft and yielding power of the Tao, or the Way, and the Taoist body (expressed especially in Tai Chi or *taijiquan*) that overwhelms and undermines the hard and rigid body of the machine. For the Taoist the body and the earth are consanguineous and conterminous because they are united and enlivened by the same energy flow, or *Ch'i*. *Ch'i* or matter/energy is central to a Taoist view of the body and of the earth, the body of the earth. *Ch'i* flows through the earth like energy through the body. In Chinese cosmology the body and the earth are both made of the same living, vital breath, or *Ch'i*. *Ch'i* is linked to water which is both the lifeblood of the earth and the major component of the human body. The same *ch'i* is pumped and flows through our veins and arteries, airways and lungs, as flows through the rest of nature. Yet Taoism is not alone in figuring the body as earth, and its fluids as water. In pre-modern western medicine the body is figured as earth and the earth as body, whereas in modern western medicine the body is figured as machine. Leonardo da Vinci (1452-1519CE) figured the body in terms of both. He is on the cusp of this transition. The diabolic genius of da Vinci was not only to propound this view of the body as earth or landscape, but also to combine it with the view of the body as machine. The sacred genius of Lao Tzu and Kuan Tzu was to propound the view of the body as earth with its flows of water, the lifeblood of the earth.

In the late 1970s I discovered Taoism, or perhaps Taoism discovered me. It was a mutual encounter anyway. I bought and read Jane English's and Giu-Fu Feng's beautifully presented translation of the *Tao te ching*, the most famous text of Taoism. I had earlier read Alan Watts' *The way of Zen* with its admirable first chapter on 'The philosophy of the Tao.' This chapter is still probably the best short introduction to Taoism. Watts followed this up with his book on Taoism (and water), *The watercourse way*. In 1980 I moved to Sydney to undertake a Master of Arts degree at Sydney University. I read a review of Geoff Pike's book, *The power of chi*, published in Sydney and I bought a copy in Sydney's Chinatown. This was my first introduction and exposure to Tai Chi. I did some of the exercises in the book over the next couple of years, but gradually realised I needed to find classes and a teacher of Tai Chi. In 1982 I moved back to Perth to do a PhD at Murdoch University. I lived in South Fremantle and saw classes in Taoist Tai Chi advertised at the Beacon Yoga Centre just around the corner and up the road. I could not believe my good fortune to find Taoism and Tai Chi combined, and classes in it available so close. I went along and joined in, and I have been doing Taoist Tai Chi ever since. Heath Greville was my teacher, hence the dedication of this book to her. Eight years later she was also my teacher of Lok Hup Ba Fa (Lui Ha Ba Fa), an older Taoist art.

Heath's teacher was Master Moy Lin-Shin, the founder of the Taoist Tai Chi Society and Gei Pang Lok Hup Academy, and the co-founder of the Fung Loy Kok Institute of Taoism, hence the dedication of *Health Recovery* to him. I was immensely privileged and fortunate to attend many workshops that Mister Moy held in Fremantle during the 1990s. I am deeply grateful to him for teaching these arts to Heath and to her for passing them on to me as they have certainly helped me to improve and maintain good health and fitness. I am also deeply grateful to him for teaching Taoist meditation to Ross Anderson and to Ross for passing this art on to me as it has certainly helped me in the most stressful and traumatic periods of my life.

I graduated from Murdoch University in 1988. Now that I had my 'driver's licence' as a researcher I started wondering what I was going to research next. It didn't take long to find a topic. In 1984 I had moved from South Fremantle to Forrestdale to build a house and live by Forrestdale Lake. The water in the lake is home to nuisance, non-biting midges. The males swarm in large numbers and made a barbecue impossible in summer. It is the god-given right of every true-blue dinkum Australian to be able to have a barbecue, but the midges, and the lake, were denying the exercise of that right. Local meetings were held to call for action, such as spraying, to kill the midges. Some people at these meetings wanted to fill in the lake and make football fields out of it. One guy even threatened to dump a 44-gallon drum of dieseline into it. I started wondering why some people hated swamps and other wetlands. This was a research question that I then researched and answered in the book, *Postmodern wetlands: Culture History Ecology* (Giblett 1996). This book could not help but touch on water, but Taoism was tangential to its concern with wetlands in European and American culture and in Australian indigenous and colonial cultures.

At the same time as I was researching and writing this book, I was becoming aware of other wetlands in Western Australia and how they were regarded in a similar way to Forrestdale Lake. I also started wanting to present wetlands in a positive light without denying or repressing their negative connotations and bad press. I was working at Murdoch University as a tutor after I finished my PhD and I shared an office with Hugh Webb who taught Aboriginal literature. We started discussing wetlands and comparing and contrasting how they are regarded across indigenous and settler cultures. We decided we could research and write a really good book on Western Australian wetlands. We then applied for funding from the Indian Ocean Centre for Peace Studies, from Murdoch University and from Curtin University where I had taken up a lectureship in 1991. This funding enabled us to travel to all the Ramsar convention wetlands of international importance in WA. We also had sufficient funding to enable a photographer, Simon Neville, to travel with us and photograph some of these wetlands. We wrote much of a book manuscript and collected stories and poems to go into it as well. We then applied for funding from the Lotteries Commission and ALCOA to publish the book, *Western Australian wetlands: The Kimberley and south-west* (Giblett and Webb 1996). It is still the only book on the subject and it touched on water too, especially in Mary Durack's classic of pastoralist literature, *Kings in grass castles*, and includes a chart and discussion of a colonial hierarchical taxonomy of water. This chapter was reprinted in *People and places of nature and culture* (Giblett, 2011). This is a general book about nature, culture, landscape aesthetics, wilderness, the bush, national parks, mining and Aboriginal country. Taoism was again tangential to its concern with wetlands in Western Australian indigenous and colonial cultures.

In 2005 I was invited to participate in the 'Water Justice' Symposium in Adelaide. This gave me the opportunity to consider what could be called 'the cross-cultural colour-coding' of water as different cultures have different coding for different colours of water. I presented a paper at the Symposium which was then published in a slightly edited (or censored) form with the title of 'Black and White Water' (Giblett, 2007, pp.31-43). The unexpurgated version was then republished as 'Black and White Water: The cross-cultural colour-coding of the life-blood of the earth-body' (Giblett, 2009). As I was considering the colour-coding and cultural valuation of water in Australian Aboriginal and colonial cultures, the Taoist view of water was certainly tangential.

Having now lived in Forrestdale for 20 years and been involved in local conservation issues and projects with the Friends of Forrestdale, I got involved in a local oral and natural history project to record and conserve the memories of former past residents and present long-time residents. The Friends group was successful in gaining funding to have an oral environmental historian, Cath Drake, record interviews with these people and to have the interviews transcribed. Fortunately, Edith Cowan University, where I had been working since 1997, granted me study leave in 2003 to write up these interviews into a book, *Forrestdale: People and place* (Giblett 2006) with funding from the Lotteries Commission. This book has a chapter on water from the point of view of the residents. Taoism was again tangential, though some residents talked about water in an implicitly Taoist way.

In 2003 I was also granted study leave to research and write a book about Taoist Tai Chi. I wanted to document the health benefits that some people gained from doing Taoist Tai Chi. Edith Cowan

University funded my study leave and travel to Canada where I interviewed a number of people who do this 'style' or 'form' of Tai Chi. After returning home, I transcribed the interviews and then wrote them up into the thematically-structured book, *Health recovery: The* Taoist Tai Chi™ *way* (Giblett 2008b) and launched by Helen Marshall at the Fremantle Arts Centre in June of that year. This book makes no mention of water, but it has a lovely photograph on the cover of a statue of Guan Yin, the Buddhist Goddess of compassion, standing on a platform overlooking a placid pond in the grounds of the International Taoist Tai Chi centre in Canada. This photo is the screen saver on my computer as I sit writing this. It sums up and expresses the calmness and calming quality of still and reflective water.

My interest in, and practice of, Tai Chi sparked a more general interest in the human body. I started researching and writing on this topic when I was at Curtin University in the early 1990s. At Edith Cowan University I had the opportunity to teach this material on several occasions. This work resulted in the book, *The body of nature and culture* (Giblett 2008a). In the previous books on wetlands I had never got around to addressing directly and extensively the Taoist understanding of water so now is the time and this is the place. The watercourse way has brought me back to water and to this place, and to this element or phase of both Chinese and European philosophy.

The *Tao te ching* contains two explicit and important mentions of water, the first in verse 8:

> The best way to live
>
>> is to be like water
>
> For water benefits all things
>
>> and goes against none of them
>
> It provides for all people
>
>> and even cleanses those places
>
>> a man is loath to go

In this way it is just like the Tao (Lao Tzu, 2001, p.21)

One of the places where 'a man is loath to go' is wetlands. Yet wetlands are a place where water already is. How can water cleanse a place where water already is? That is part of the paradox of water – and the Tao. It is already in places where a man is loath to go and it cleanses those places. Or perhaps more precisely, the plants of the place absorb the nutrients and filter the water to make it cleansing. This water provides for all people and benefits all things. It thus gives an exemplar of the way to live. By going low, by going to low places, by taking the lower part, by going into the nether lands and into the grotesque lower bodily and earthly regions, water not only goes to places men are loath to go but also cleanses, provides and benefits all people and all things (see Giblett, 1996, 2008a).

The other mention of water in the *Tao te ching* in verse 78 also highlights the paradoxical power of water – and the Tao:

> Nothing in the world
>
> > is as soft and yielding as water
>
> Yet for attacking the hard and strong
>
> > none can triumph so easily
>
> It is weak, yet none can equal it
>
> It is soft, yet none can damage it
>
> It is yielding, yet none can wear it away
>
> Everyone knows that the soft overcomes the hard
>
> and the yielding triumphs over the rigid (Lao Tzu, 2001, p.91)

The rock wears away from water flowing over it, but the water never wears. Water is the wearing agent. Water exemplifies the soft and yielding power of the Tao, and of the Taoist body (expressed especially in Tai Chi or *taijiquan*), that overwhelms and undermines the hard and rigid body of the machine (expressed especially in the Fascist body and body-building; see Giblett, 2008a).

The slow, graceful movements of *taijiquan* are like a gently flowing river; the stillness in movement and the movement in stillness of *taijiquan* are like the still waters of a wooded wetland reflecting the heavens above; the moving meditation of *taijiquan* is like a deep ocean pool full of waving and weaving mysteries; the power and grace of *taijiquan* is like a serpentine stream curving and straightening through the body of the earth; the strength and flexibility of the Taoist body in *taijiquan* is like a continental river with deep currents carrying mighty ships and with shallow billabongs giving birth, nutrition and shelter to small fish; the internal circulation of energy in the body in the practise of *taijiquan* is like a underground stream coursing through the cavities and waters of the lower earthly stratum cleansing and purifying them; the rising of energy from the feet, through the pelvis and up the spine to the top of the head in *taijiquan* is like a bubbling spring welling up from deep underground to bathe the brain, the 'palace of the mud ball,' in cerebro-spinal fluid; the internal alchemy of *taijiquan* rejuvenates like a delta or lagoon giving birth to new life, the most fertile places on the planet; the generating and storing of energy, the accumulation of *chi,* in *taijiquan* is like an estuary to which all good things flow and which expels bad things; *yin* and *yang* complementing each other are like the black waters of slimy swamps and the white waters of mountain streams, both part of the body of the earth — the Tao is like water.

In his notes to verse 78 of *Tao te ching* Jonathan Star elaborates that:

> although each element of nature can be likened to the Absolute, water has always been the most endeared by the Taoist and the one closest to the nature of Tao. Water not only represents humility, gentleness, and a mind in perfect repose, but it is the element that gives birth to all life. Witness this brilliant passage on water from the *Kuan-tzu* – a Taoist work of the fourth century B.C.E:

> water is the blood of the Earth; it flows through its muscles and veins. . . It is accumulated in Heaven and Earth and

stored up in the various things of the world. It comes forth in metal and stone and is concentrated in living creatures. Therefore it is said that water is something with a spirit. Being accumulated in plants and trees, their stems gain orderly progression, their flowers obtain proper number, and their fruit gain proper measure. Water gathers in jade, and the nine virtues appear. It congeals to form man. . . that is its most refined essence. . . Nothing is produced without it. Only he who knows how to rely on its principles can act correctly. (Lao Tzu, 2001, p.269)

For the Taoist, the earth is a body and water is the life-blood of the earth.

Moreover, for the Taoist, as Allan (1997, p.4) puts it, water 'is the model for philosophical ideas about the nature of the cosmos.' It is also the model for personal conduct and for life itself. The Classical Chinese word, *shui*, conventionally translated as 'water' is thus, Allan (1997, p.32) argues, 'a broader category than the English "water".' Confucius (cited by Allan, 1997, p.24) said that 'water, which extends everywhere and gives everything life without acting (*wuwei*) is like virtue (*de*) . . . Its bubbling up, never running dry, is like the way (*dao*).' Water is thus the model for three of the central concepts of Confucianism and Taoism: the *dao* or *tao*, the way, itself; *de*, virtue; and *wuwei*, nonaction. For Allan (1997, p.31):

> water served as a root metaphor in the formulation of abstract concepts that were the basis of the system of social and ethical values.

It also served in the same capacity in relation to environmental and corporeal values, and to the earth and the body.

The Taoists are concerned with 'the flow of energy in the land' (Wong, 2001, p.122). The ancient Taoist art of *feng shui* is concerned, as Skinner (1989, p.xi) puts it, 'with the location of dragon lines [or veins (Wong, 1996, pp.30 and 65-68; see also Wong, 2001, p.136)] of energy in the earth and their interaction with man [*sic*] as part of his subtle environment.' For Cheng (1994, p.123) 'dragon arteries wind through the landscape' or more precisely, as landscape is a surface phenomenon (see Giblett, 2004), they wind through the land, both its surface and depth. In Chinese languages, as Allan (1997, p.56) points out, 'there is no word for landscape as such.' Landscape is a western category that colonises the land conceptually and concretely (see Giblett, 2011).

In Chinese terms energy or 'life-force' is *ch'i* that 'flows through the earth like an underground stream' (Skinner, 1989, p.1). *Ch'i* also flows through the earth like energy through the body. Thus for Skinner (1989, p.1) 'a parallel can be drawn with the flow of *ch'i* through the acupuncture meridians through the body.' Conversely, a parallel can be drawn with the flow of energy through the earth. *Feng-shui* is a kind of ecological *taijiquan* as Wong (1996, p.46) defines it as 'the art of seeing the pattern of movement and stillness in the land' just as *tajiquani* is the art of performing movement with, and cultivating stillness in, the body. Acupuncture, *feng-shui* and *tai c'hi* are Taoist arts of health, longevity and well-being for the body and the earth, for the body of the earth.

The body and the earth form the body of the earth, what Rossbach (1984, p.8) calls 'a sacred metabolic system' of energy flows in living beings, rather than the secular metabolic exchange of dead matter in modern industrial capitalism (see Giblett, 2008a, chapter 1). Whereas the former is enacted in the cultivation and circulation of energy in the living body of the earth, the latter culminates in the production of the commodity and in the exchange of dead matter and labour for money, and of money for dead matter. And whereas the latter gives rise to nature as 'man's [*sic*] inorganic body' from which 'he' is alienated and on which 'he' works in the production of commodities, the former is intimately related to nature as humans' body with which humans are united and (with) which humans work (see Giblett, 2008a, 2011).

For the Taoist the body and the earth are consanguineous and conterminous because they are united and enlivened by the same energy flow, or *Ch'i*. *Ch'i* or matter/energy is central to a Taoist view of the body and of the earth, the body of the earth. *Ch'i* for Wei-Ming (1989, p.76) is 'the blood and breath of the vital force that underlies all beings.' The *Guanzi (Chuang Tzu)* calls water 'the blood and breath of the earth' (cited by Kurijama, 1999, p.50). *Ch'i/qi*, or vitality as Allan (1997, p.60) as translates it, is 'closely associated with breath – and mist, the breath of the earth. . . and in later theory it is said to be that which everything is made of.' For Cheng (1994, p.117) 'the vital breaths simultaneously animate both the being of the universe and the being of man [*sic*].' One breath, two beings: human being and the being of the universe are distinct and not merged into one whole but breathe the same breath.

Ch'i/qi contrasts with some major western concepts, such as matter. *Ch'i/qi,* according to Graham (cited by Allan, 1997 p.88) occupies:

> The place in Chinese cosmology occupied by matter in ours. The basic metaphor behind the word matter is of timber (Latin *materia*), inert and cut up and to be assembled by a carpenter; *qi*, on the other hand, is in the first place breath, alternating between motion and stillness.

This alternation between motion and stillness is expressed in *taiiquan*. *Taijiquan* involves what Mauss (1992, p.469) calls 'dancing at rest;' it is also what he calls 'a technique of active rest.' The techniques of active rest, such as *taiiquan,* can be contrasted with the techniques of passive speed of modern communication and transportation technologies (see Gblettt, 2008b).

In Maussian terms the narrator in Julia Kristeva's (1992, p.169) novel *The Samurai* describes *taijiquan* as 'a kind of tortoiselike eurythmics.' One character goes on to elaborate in Maussian terms that in *taijiquan*:

> You dance with your arteries and veins . . . – it's not a matter of arms and legs. Your blood surges forward, draws back, and then the time comes when your body's transformed. It doesn't disappear, but the rhythm of your blood is in harmony with shapes you imagine in space – your body itself

is all space, what's inside and outside are brought together and redistributed, magnified almost to infinity, anatomised to infinity.

Taijiquan is an external and internal dance of bodily limbs, organs and fluids choreographed to the imagined shapes and actions of animal movements: stork cools wings, snake creeps down, golden cock stands on one leg, and so on. Every activity of the Taoist body, and not only *taijiquan*, is, in Kohn's (1991, p.229) terms, 'patterned on the rhythm of the world at large.'

In Chinese cosmology the body and the earth are both made of the same living, vital breath (see Cheng, 1986, pp.362-363). In western cosmology the body and the earth are both made of the same inert and desiccated matter. Matter is dry whereas breath is wet. Blood is wet too, and so *ch'i/qi* is linked to it, and both are linked to water, which is the life-blood of the earth and the major component of the human body. Water in the *Guanzi* is 'the blood and *qi*-breath of the earth' (cited by Allan, 1997, p.123). Conversely, *qi* is the water and breath of the body. Consequently for Wei-Ming (1989, p.78) 'we are consanguineous with nature.' We share the same blood, and breath, of *ch'i* as nature. The same *ch'i* is pumped and flows through our veins and arteries, airways and lungs, as flows through the rest of nature. Interestingly, in the theory of the four elements (and humours) in western philosophy air and the gaseous are associated with the wet and sanguineous (see Giblett, 1996, pp.156-160).

The *ch'i* in the plural for Graham (1989, p.325) are 'the energetic fluids in the atmosphere and inside the body.' They are not a singular substance and they are not confined to a single, self-contained entities but run through the body and the earth. The *Chuang-tzu* states that 'running through the whole world there is nothing but the one *ch'i*' (quoted by Graham 1989, p.328). *Ch'i* for Sullivan (1962, p.7) is 'the breath of the universe.' The idea of breath for Cheng (1994, p.118) 'is at the core of Chinese cosmology,' including traditional medicine. Indeed, medicine is a part of cosmology as Cheng goes on to argue that 'every living thing is primarily conceived not as a mere substance but as a condensation of the different types of breaths that regulate its vital functioning.'

In Chinese cosmology and medicine the kidneys are associated with water (Wong, 2000, pp. 61, 69 and 119). The kidneys are the place or organ where *ch'i* is generated and stored (Wong, 2000, pp. 96-7 and 102). Correspondingly, wetlands as the 'kidneys' of the earth are the site or 'organ' where the life-giving vitality of water is generated and stored. Both are places of the life-giving flow of water, not of foul stagnancy. In Chinese cosmology and medicine the liver is associated with wood and 'in wood the sap must flow' (Hammer, 1990, p.57) or else the tree will die just as in the body of the earth water must flow or the earth will die. The liver energies, Hammer (1990, p.64) goes on to relate, 'play a major part in the movement and circulation of *ch'i* and the prevention of stagnation.' Although wetlands have been regarded as stagnant, they are dynamic systems often of subsurface water flows. They are vital for life. Like wetlands, the kidneys for Chung (Wong, 2000, p.121) are 'the root and foundation of life.' The human body and the body of the earth are connected in and by the life-giving movement of energy.

Taoism is not alone in figuring the body as earth, and its fluids as water. In pre-modern western medicine the body is figured as earth and the earth as body, whereas in modern western medicine the body is figured as machine. Leonardo da Vinci (1452-1519) figured the body in terms of both. He is on the cusp of this transition. For him, the human body is a sort of microcosm of both the machine and the earth, and the earth the macrocosm of the human body:

> While man [*sic*] has within himself bones as a stay and framework for the flesh, the world has stones which are supports of earth. While man has within him a pool of blood wherein the lungs as he breathes expand and contract, so the body of the earth has its ocean, which also rises and falls every six hours with the breathing of the world; as from the said pool of blood proceed the veins which spreads their branches through the human body, so the ocean fills the body of the

earth with an infinite number of veins of water... In this body of the earth is lacking, however, the nerves, and these are absent because nerves are made for the purpose of movement; and as the world is perpetually stable, and no movement takes place here, nerves are not necessary. But in all other things man and the earth are very much alike. (da Vinci, 1977, pp.45,6)

On this view, the body of the earth (the body and the earth) is inert, motionless, passive and unmoving, despite the lungs contracting and expanding and the pool of blood ebbing and flowing in Leonardo's pre-'heart as pump' view of the circulation of blood. These are counter-balanced movements, or actions and reactions that are not particularly purposive; they just occur and recur in homeostasis.

The only difference for Leonardo between the body and the earth is that in his view the earth does not have nerves to make it move whereas the body has. Interestingly, the development of telegraphy using wires and cables, and radio using the electromagnetosphere, were later figured in terms of an earthly nervous system. Conversely, the bodily nervous system, or at least what Breuer called 'the paths of connection and conduction in the brain,' could be figured as an electrical system that supplied both light and power to the rest of the body. What Breuer (1893/2004,[1] p.197) went to call on 'a cerebral path of conduction' should not be pictured 'as a telephone line that is excited electrically only when operating' but as 'an electrical system with many different branches for supplying light and transmitting motor power.' Modern industrial technology gave nerves to the earth and an electrical system to the body that both otherwise lacked. Like the nervous system, telegraphy and radio were the control system that coordinated the movements of empires and corporations. Telecommunications and the Internet perform the same function today of a command and control nervous system for international trade and transnational corporations (see Giblett, 2008b).

---

[1] All these aspects mentioned in this paragraph receive a systematic, often chapter-by-chapter discussion in Giblett (2008a). See also Giblett (2009, pp.151-152).

Although Leonardo does not explicitly mention the machine, it is implicit in the idea that the body is a passive assemblage of parts (anatomy) until and unless it is acted upon by the nervous system and made to move and function (physiology). The editor of a selection from Leonardo's notebooks argues that he 'looked upon anatomy with the eye of a mechanician' (in da Vinci, 1977, p.150).

> Leonardo also looked upon geology and geography with the eye of a mechanician. In a similar vein, Kenneth Clark (1939, p.175) comments that, to Leonardo a landscape, like a human being, was part of a vast machine, to be understood part by part and, if possible, in the whole. Rocks were not simply decorative silhouettes. They were part of the earth's bones, with an anatomy of their own, caused by some remote seismic upheaval.

To Leonardo the whole could be taken apart to be understood part by part without necessarily understanding, or leading to an understanding of, the whole. Water was not simply a pool of fluid but was part of the earth's blood with a physiology of its own caused by the shape and lie of the land, its topography, or anatomy. Both the human body and the body of the earth have veins as Leonardo suggests. Both the landscape and the body is a machine composed of parts. The body is figured as earth, but both are figured as machine. The machine is the master trope that serves equally well for the body and the earth.

In drawing in two senses a parallel between the body and the earth Leonardo was not simply and unthinkingly following convention but deliberately setting up an explanatory device. Introducing a series of his drawings, Leonardo announced that:

> In fifteen entire figures there shall be revealed to you the microcosm on the same plan as before me was adopted by Ptolemy in his cosmography; and I shall divide them into limbs as he divided the macrocosm into provinces; and I shall then define the functions of the parts in every direction, placing before your eyes the representation of the whole

figure of man and his capacity of movements by means of his parts. (da Vinci, 1977, p152)

'Man' moves by means of his parts but these parts are coordinated into a whole. If the parts were to move independently, the whole would wracked by them moving in contrary directions and they would be torn apart. By constituting 'man' as made up of parts, Leonardo has reduced the body to machine, not only in the structure of its parts, its anatomy, but also in the functioning of its parts, its physiology. This view persisted through the nineteenth century when physiology, for Thomas Huxley, is 'the mechanical engineering of living machines.'

By performing the function of eating, the alimentary and digestive parts of the machine are put to work in transforming dead matter into living organism:

> Man and animals are really the passage and conduit of food, the sepulchre of animals and resting-place of the dead, making life out of the death of the other (taking pleasure in the misery of others), making themselves the covering for corruption. (da Vinci, 1977, p. 278)

Beneath the skin, the skull lies. The skull beneath the skin is a traditional Christian reminder of death. The human body for Leonardo is a cloak for death and a reminder of death, a *memento mori*. It is a sadistic device for taking pleasure from other's pain. It is a machine for making life out of death. Yet, as I have argued elsewhere (see Giblett, 1996), the body is both a tomb and a womb. The body is both crucifixion and resurrection, mass and transubstantiation, the transformation of the dead elements of bread and wine into the living body, the alchemy of the dross of dead matter into the gold of living being. 'Man' is a secular Christ; Renaissance humanism, a secular theology.

If the body is machine, the doctor is a mechanic, and medicine is servicing, tuning and repairing the machine (see Stibbe, 1996, p.186). For da Vinci (1977, p. 279) 'medicine is the restoration of discordant elements; sickness is the discord of the elements infused into the living body.' From where do the discord of the elements come to be infused into the living body? It comes from the body of the earth, from the mixing of elements in the body of the earth (see Giblett, 1996, chapter 5). How do discordant elements come to be infused into the human body? Through the nose and the mouth principally, those orifices through which what is outside is taken inside.

Leonardo was not alone in the Renaissance in espousing the worldview of the body as earth, and the earth as body. Walter Raleigh in his *History of the World* propounded the view that:

> his [*sic*] blood, which disperseth itself by the branches of veins through all the body, may be resembled to those waters which are carried by brooks and rivers over all the earth, his breath to the air, his natural heat to the inclosed warmth which the earth hath in itself. . . our eyes to the light of the sun and the moon. (cited in Tillyard, 1943, p.99)

The diabolic genius of da Vinci was not only to propound this view of the body as earth or landscape, but also to combine it with the view of the body as machine. The sacred genius of Lao Tzu and Kuan Tzu was to propound the view of the body as earth with its flows of water, the lifeblood of the earth.

5. THE WAY OF TAOIST TAI CHI

The ancient Chinese art of Tai Chi is now widely recognised in western, industrialised countries and some of its benefits are readily acknowledged. The slow, graceful movements of Tai Chi are so well-known that they are occasionally used in television advertisements often just to signify relaxation or a healthy life-style. Tai Chi is visually appealing and people who watch it often remark that it looks relaxing. More importantly, the people who do it often say that it feels relaxing, and that it is relaxing too.

Many people will have heard that Tai Chi is good for relieving arthritis, or for improving balance, or reducing high blood pressure, or preventing osteoporosis, or helping with a range of other conditions. People who do, practice or play Taoist Tai Chi sometimes have these, or other, incurable or terminal, conditions such as Lou Gehrig's syndrome, Multiple Sclerosis, Cerebral Palsy, Alzheimer's, or have had cancer or a stroke. *Health Recovery: The Taoist Tai Chi™ Way* (Giblett, 2008b). presents the stories of some people who have some of these conditions. Other people start doing Taoist Tai Chi because they are unfit and want to get fit; overweight and want to lose weight; and even because they are healthy and want to stay healthy, especially as they get older.

There are no miraculous cures to be had through the practice of Taoist Tai Chi, but there can be, and are, remarkable transformational experiences and big improvements in functionality, even with the simple practices of everyday life which many of us take for granted such as walking, and even standing; in balance, strength and flexibility; and in a general sense of wellbeing, and so improved quality of life and increased length of life.

Tai Chi is taught in a number of 'styles' or traditions. Taoist Tai Chi emphasises the health-restoring and -maintaining aspects of Tai Chi and other Taoist arts of health and well-being. Health-improvement is one of the aims of the Taoist Tai Chi Society. Health, however, is not defined in *Health Recovery* (nor by the Society, I would suggest) in narrow, physical terms, but in broad, holistic terms that include physical, mental, spiritual, emotional, and even environmental health. Taoist Tai Chi focuses on the physical as the initial means to gain health in the other areas as well. Change the body to change the mind and spirit is a motto of the tradition of Taoism from which Taoist Tai Chi and the Society come.

Taoist Tai Chi has a variety of specific and demonstrable benefits. It is described in an old brochure published by the Taoist Tai Society of Australia as:

> a gentle art of health for people of all ages and health conditions. The slow, graceful movements of Taoist Tai Chi increase strength and flexibility and improve balance and circulation. The Taoist style of Tai Chi emphasises stretching and turning in each of the movements in order to gain these and other benefits more effectively.

The brochure goes on to relate that:

> Regular practice of Taoist Tai Chi can bring a wide range of health benefits to the muscular, skeletal and circulatory systems. The flowing movements of Taoist Tai Chi serve as a moving meditation that reduces stress and provides a way to cultivate body and mind. Specific health benefits include:
>
> - toning of muscles, tendons and other soft tissues;
> - rotation of the joints through a full range of motion;
> - stretching and alignment of the spine to make it strong and supple;
> - gentle massage of the internal organs to improve their functioning.

Taoist Tai Chi was developed by Master Moy Lin-Shin (1931-1998) and brought to the west in 1970 when he founded the Taoist Tai Chi Society. Since then the Society has grown to be the largest non-profit, volunteer Tai Chi organization in the world. Taoist Tai Chi is practiced in over 25 countries and 500 locations around the world, mainly in Europe, North America and Australia.

As Master Moy founded the Society, his teaching and vision are the source of those benefits, including the health benefits. Tracing the lineage of Taoist Tai Chi and the Society back to its source in Master Moy is not only the respectful thing to do, but also establishes the legitimacy and power of the practice and its health benefits. It is an important aspect of Taoist Tai Chi, and of the ongoing teaching of it, that an accomplished master taught it initially and did so for many years. The students of Master Moy hold him in great respect.

Master Moy, however, was not your stereotype of the guru who dressed flashily, drove a big car and lived a lavish lifestyle. He usually wore a Taoist Tai Chi tee-shirt and a track-suit with the Society logo on it. He never took a salary and he lived a very simple life. He also did not adopt the master position in which he was the all-seeing, all-knowing master on to whom the student transferred their desires and fears.

Besides founding the Society and being the source of Taoist Tai Chi and other arts of health and well-being, Master Moy also taught chanting and meditation. The Society offers instruction and practice in both at some locations as part of the Taoist lineage and heritage. These health-improving practices are complementary with the other arts and integral to the activities of the Society, to the process of health recovery and to stories about it as collected for, and discussed in, *Health Recovery*.

The Society is largely an oral culture where its activities take place in a face-to-face situation, including learning Taoist Tai Chi. In fact, it is recommended that everyone learns in a class, and not from a book or video. It is difficult, if not impossible, to learn from a book or video, though the Society has both available as they have a useful function to provide aids to memory about moves, and the sequence of moves, taught in a class. *Health Recovery*, by contrast, tries to give a sense of the oral culture of the Society by presenting stories about it.

These stories are excerpted from transcriptions of interviews, an oral genre. Of course, *Health Recovery* is a written account, too, like illness narratives. It is thus a pale imitation of actually talking to the people who told their stories initially face-to-face. Hopefully, though, it tells their stories adequately and gives a sense of their experience, and of the oral culture of the Society. A number of men and women, of different ages, from a variety of backgrounds, of various nationalities, in good or poor health (or somewhere between them) tell their stories. These stories show that Taoist Tai Chi is not just for the old or young, mobile or immobile, sick or ill, fit or unfit. It is for everybody. What other activity or club has members that range in age from 9 to 90, from those in the pink of health to those on death's door, from those who cannot feed themselves, stand up or walk unaided to those who do rolls, splits and headstands? And all this is done in a friendly, non-competitive and supportive environment?

Setting

The rolling hills of rural Ontario in Canada are the perfect location for the International Health Recovery Centre of the Taoist Tai Chi Society. It is located in the Mono area near Orangeville, about a 35-40 minute drive north-west of Toronto. The peaceful atmosphere of the Centre and its grounds provide an ideal, and idyllic, retreat and refuge for people to focus and work on regaining and improving their health. The property is about 106 acres in size. It includes a secluded wood through which the Bruce Trail wends on its way from Niagara Falls to the tip of Bruce Peninsula.

I visited this Centre and stayed there for 6 weeks from July to September in 2003 when I was on Study Leave from Edith Cowan University in Perth, Western Australia. I also made a brief visit to the Taoist Tai Chi Society of the USA Centre in Tallahassee, Florida. The Orangeville Centre in Canada is unique and its work is invaluable (and all royalties from the sale of *Health Recovery* go to help support it). It provides rich opportunities for research into Taoist Tai Chi not available elsewhere in the world as nothing like this Centre exists anywhere else. *Health Recovery* presents to outsiders for the first time insiders' stories about the Centre and the Society.

I visited the centre at Orangeville much like an anthropologist visits a remote tribe, studies their practices, rituals and life-ways, and then brings home the booty in the form of an ethnographic study comprising knowledge of that other culture. It is as if there is this strange tribe scattered around the world whose members practice some aspects of the ancient Chinese arts of healing. Generally members of the tribe have jobs and families, but occasionally some of them come to their Centre in Canada to work together intensively on their own Tai Chi, to improve their health, and to teach and help others. I wanted to study the life and activities of this Centre and concentrate on the community and culture of Taoist Tai Chi and of the Society, and only focus on individuals as the bearers of knowledge and as informants about both. The aim was not to showcase or privilege the experience of those individuals, but to use it as a means of presenting the culture and community of Taoist Tai Chi and the Society as the context for health recovery and stories about it.

Of course, in the case of this ethnographic study, as a member of the Taoist Tai Chi Society and instructor of Taoist Tai Chi myself I belong in some sense to the same (modern, western) culture and (Taoist Tai Chi) 'tribe.' Yet there are cultural differences between the various classes outlined above and between Canada and the US to which I travelled and Australia from where I came. I acknowledge and respect these differences and reflected critically on the process of the research, including in both recording observations and conducting interviews. As a member of the same 'tribe' (albeit in a remote location in Australia) I was not a dispassionate observer, but rather a participant observer conducting fieldwork in a semi-familiar place. It was familiar in the sense that the people did Taoist Tai Chi like me; unfamiliar in the sense that they were doing it in Ontario and Florida in two countries (and indeed in a hemisphere) that I had not visited before. In technical terms, I was doing ethnography from within (if that is possible).

My function as ethnographer was to engage in dialogue with the interviewees and to allow them to tell their own stories. My role as writer has been to make observations, draw conclusions, avoid editorialising and generally let the storytellers speak directly to the reader without interruption. My position as author is not that of an objective reporter, but of an engaged advocate. I was too implicated and involved as an instructor of Taoist Tai Chi and office bearer of the Society, and had been for too long, to try to, or to pretend to, stand outside it and observe it from that point of view. *Health Recovery* is for outsiders with insiders' stories by an insider. For those who are interested, I reflect more on these aspects, and in more academic terms, in the final chapter of *Health Recovery*.

Being a participant-observer was certainly the case during the first week I was at the Orangeville Centre. I arrived just before a five-day Health Recovery Program commenced. The Administrator of the Centre, Kelly Ekman and the Medical Director, Dr Bruce McFarlane, asked me to be a Participant for this week so that I could become familiar with a Health Recovery program. I attended two subsequent Health Recovery weeks, the next one as an Assistant and the final one as the researcher (and amateur photographer) for *Health Recovery*. Through this process I was able to learn about the operations of the Centre and the activities of a Health Recovery Program from the point of view of both a Participant and an Assistant. I was also able to make contact and develop trust with potential storytellers. I also kept a journal in which I made observations about the life, activities and people of the Centre, including some of the storytellers. Some of these observations are presented in the final chapter of *Health Recovery*.

How did I choose the storytellers? Or how did they choose to become involved? The 'sample' selected is not random, though it is rather arbitrary. I wanted to interview a broad range of people on the continuums of age, health and mobility as I have indicated. There was a touch of serendipity to it. Some people who told me their stories I had met only 5 minutes before. Others had become friends over several weeks, and occasionally months, of doing Taoist Tai Chi together, eating meals together, washing dishes together and enjoying conversation. The Centre at Orangeville is like that. People live together, work together, do Tai Chi together and share the common tasks of everyday life together. And have a lot of fun and laugh a lot doing them. Generally the storytellers were interested in the project and wanted to help out. Taoist Tai Chi people are like that. Sometimes I had heard that they had an interesting or remarkable story to tell that others should hear. At other times I didn't know much about them at all. Our paths crossed and we stopped for a chat that was recorded and later transcribed, some bits of which made their way into *Health Recovery*.

Health Recovery is a kind of photo album of snapshots showing people in certain places at particular times talking about their experience of doing Taoist Tai Chi and being members of the Society or participants in its activities. It does not pretend to be representative of all the people, and their experiences, who do Taoist Tai Chi. Yet these stories have validity in their own right, though it is not possible to extrapolate from this small sample of informants and to generalise from them about Taoist Tai Chi, the Society and its effects on people. The book aims to give a flavour of the range of what happens in the Society. If you go to these places and talk to these people, they may tell you something slightly different on any given day. If you go to these places and talk to different people, they may tell you something slightly different. If you go to different places and talk to different people, they will tell you something slightly different too. Every person's experience of doing Taoist Tai Chi is different and unique. Yet there are some commonalities and some surprising similarities between what practitioners of Taoist Tai Chi say about it, and what members of the Society say about it. Those commonalities and similarities will become apparent in more detail later.

It may be valuable at this point to indicate a common theme in order to set the scene for what follows. One of the major, common characteristics that the storytellers repeatedly talked about is the social solidarity and support that the Taoist Tai Chi Society provides to them and other members. The Society is a kind of second family and second home for many people that adds to, or replaces, their first family and home, which could be unsatisfactory or unsupportive or no longer available or in existence. This sense of community is important for improving or maintaining health and well-being. Yet the Society is not just a social club or a cult. It is the context for hard work, physical effort, spiritual nurturing and mental dedication. This holistic approach to health combines the mental, physical, social and spiritual. It gives a deeply satisfying experience and provides the opportunity for lifelong learning.

Yet the aim of *Health Recovery* is not to paint a rosy picture and create unrealistic expectations, certainly not of miraculous cures. The Society is not utopia, and Taoist Tai Chi is not a panacea, though it helps to cure many of the world's, and people's, ills. The Society is a human institution and Taoist Tai Chi is a human activity. Both are flawed and far from perfect, like all human institutions and activities. On the whole, though, you meet a great bunch of nice people who get along well with each other, and who help and support each other. Of course, there are tensions and frictions, misunderstandings and outbursts, 'personality clashes' and the occasional unseemly argument, but not a lot of bitchiness or political infighting. Those who find all this niceness too much to handle leave.

Others leave for other reasons. Some people come expecting miracle cures and don't get them; some people leave in frustration, their expectations, for whatever reason, not met; some people come to try it out and find it's not for them; some people leave because they did not realize that they would have to work so hard at it; some people come as customers to sample the wares and find that there is nothing to buy; some people come to try it because they've tried yoga, and/or boot-scooting, and/or ballroom dancing and/or Chinese cooking, so Tai Chi is next; some people leave after the novelty wears off, or it becomes too hard, or too open-ended, or whatever. Everyone is welcome to come and free to go, as signs say at some locations.

And some people come and stay, for a while at least. One person who tells their story in *Health Recovery* had only been doing Taoist Taoist Tai Chi for 5 days. Others stay for a long time, sometimes for many years, even decades. Another person who tells their story had been doing Taoist Tai Chi for 25 years. In between were those who have been doing it for varying lengths of time. Sometimes some of these people speculated occasionally on why people leave, but no one tracks them down to ask them why and most don't come back to say why. These are not their stories.

People start learning Taoist Tai Chi for a variety of reasons. Some people talk about some of their reasons for doing so. Some people are seriously ill and want to get better, or at least get no worse; other people are healthy and want to stay healthy, or improve their health. A large number of people who do Taoist Tai Chi are somewhere in between these two extremes. For many people, learning Taoist Tai Chi has also had a variety of effects, including benefits. Some people get better; some get worse; some get no worse; and some stay healthy, or even get healthier. Most people, irrespective of their condition (their health or physical condition) become fitter and stronger, more flexible, and more relaxed – and so just plain better, more healthy, human beings. When a willing participant agreed to tell their story about their experience of doing Taoist Tai Chi they began by saying why they started doing it. One of the aims of *Health Recovery* is to relate people's reasons and motivations for starting, and continuing to do, Taoist Tai Chi. After saying why they started doing it, they often go on to talk about the effects that doing it has had on them. Usually these are beneficial effects and these were the reasons for continuing.

There are some common features in people's experience of learning Taoist Tai Chi. One thing that comes up time and again is the need to take responsibility for one's own health (which is why some people come to Taoist Tai Chi in the first place). Another is the need to take responsibility for one's practice of Taoist Tai Chi (which is why some people stay with Taoist Tai Chi for the long term). Taking such responsibility is often regarded as important in the context of the current situation in the health sector in which people are being expected to take greater responsibility for their own health. It is also important for some people in terms of an individual journey to achieve health and well-being, physically, mentally and spiritually. These all require putting in the effort and doing the work in order to gain the benefits. The second aim and objective of the Society is 'to promote the health-improving qualities of Taoist Tai Chi.' Many practitioners of Taoist Tai Chi put into practice its elaboration: 'practiced diligently, Taoist Tai Chi cultivates both body and mind to restore and maintain good health.' There are no easy answers in Taoist Tai Chi and everyone who wants to experience its benefits has to work diligently and has to begin learning as a beginner. Learning Taoist Tai Chi is also part of an oral tradition and part of traditional Chinese oral culture. Learning takes place in a class, not alone, and not from a book or video. Information about classes and locations is available on the Taoist Tai Chi Society website www.taoist.org as well as information about the history of the Society and the lineage of Taoist Tai Chi.

For anyone to learn Taoist Tai Chi, there has to be a teacher of Taoist Tai Chi; for learning to occur, there has to be teaching; for anyone to experience benefits from doing the moves of Taoist Tai Chi, they have to learn and practice them; for anyone to go on learning, they need to teach, or to help teach, or to help in any way they can. Teaching Taoist Tai Chi is an integral part of the learning experience and of gaining the health benefits from doing it. The first aim and objective of the Taoist Tai Chi Society is 'to make Taoist Tai Chi available to all.' For that to happen, there has to be instructors. For a health recovery story to be told, there has to be a health recovery process, and for *that* to occur, there has to be a teacher who teaches health recovery and who enables the health recovery process to occur.

'Health Recovery' is an umbrella term that covers teaching Taoist Tai Chi and other Taoist arts of health, such as chanting and meditation, to people with a range of health conditions or illnesses. These could be chronic, long-term, debilitating, life-threatening, or terminal — or not. Health Recovery is taught either in classes at local branches of the Taoist Tai Chi Society, or in 5 day or shorter programs, at centres of the Society, such as at Orangeville. As the name implies, the aim of Health Recovery classes and programs is for the participants to recover their health. In many cases this is not possible in terms of some people recovering 'normal' health in the sense of regaining normal functionality and/or mobility. In these cases the aim of Health Recovery is to maintain as much as possible, if not improve, their current level of functionality and mobility, and so improve their quality of life. The aim for the participants is to get better and not to get worse. 'Do no harm' is the motto for the lead instructors and their assistants.

In the case of people with a terminal illness, the aim is ultimately, in the last words of Master Moy, to comfort people while they are dying and after death. One of the aims of the Taoist Tai Chi Society is for everybody to improve their health so in this sense everybody who does Taoist Tai Chi is in health recovery, hence the title of the book. And everybody who does Taoist Tai Chi has a story to tell about it. Everybody is recovering health; everybody is in the process of recovering their health.

Health Recovery Programs are the heart and soul of Taoist Tai Chi and the Taoist Tai Chi Society. They are the place where often the most remarkable recovery of health is experienced and about which the most remarkable health recovery stories are told. These Programs are made up of sustained and in-depth work on the moves of the Tai Chi set and other movements. These programs are held once a month at the Orangeville Centre, though they are sometimes available elsewhere when Kelly Ekman, the Administrator of the program, and Dr Bruce McFarlane, the Medical Director, take them on the road in eastern and western Canada. They go to the core of the practice of Taoist Tai Chi, the culture of the Society and following the Taoist virtues of exercising compassion, helping others and giving selflessly. They also go to the heart and soul of the passing on the benefits of Taoist Tai Chi, not only to the hale and hearty, but also to the sick and dying. The aim of the programs is not to cure illness, but to improve quality of life (especially functionality and mobility). The level of care and attention given by the assistants to participants who attend the live-in programs at Orangeville is quite astonishing. These are all core components of many health recovery stories.

One of the four aims of the Taoist Tai Chi Society is 'to promote cultural exchange.' A subsidiary aim is, 'through Taoist Tai Chi and other activities, . . . to make the richness of Chinese culture more accessible, and thereby promote greater understanding and respect among people.' This aim implies making the richness of traditional Chinese healing arts more accessible to everybody and to modern western medicine, and modern western society more generally. Yet this process is a two-way street with traffic going the other way through studying and understanding Taoist Tai Chi in modern western medical terms. The Society values and promotes this two-way exchange. There is a high level of interest in, and understanding of, modern western medicine in the Society.

Master Moy instigated the building of a bridge between the two cultures and their medical theories and practices so that there would be exchange between the two to their mutual benefit, and to people's benefit ultimately. He was personally interested in modern western anatomy and physiology. He encouraged the understanding of Taoist Tai Chi and the other Taoist arts in western medical terms. He appointed western medical advisors to the Society who led workshops that focussed on Taoist Tai Chi and anatomy or physiology. He asked them to give lectures and write articles on Taoist Tai Chi and anatomy or physiology for the Society, its newsletters and its members. He was not seeking the legitimation of Taoist Tai Chi through modern western medicine as it has its own legitimacy and efficacy as we have seen in previous chapters. Rather, he was seeking to understand, and to promote the understanding, of Taoist Tai Chi in modern western medical terms, and to develop the interest of western medical and health theorists and practitioners in Taoist Tai Chi. Out of this exchange a richer, broader health and medical practice has been developed, at least within the Society, for its members and for practitioners of Taoist Tai Chi, that includes both, or the best of both cultural practices, and that prevents or lessens the incidence or severity of illness or other health conditions and improves health. This chapter continues that legacy of his and furthers the aim of the Society to promote cultural exchange, especially in the area of health promotion and health communication.

The cross-cultural dialogue and exchange set up by Master Moy, and continued by the Taoist Tai Chi Society, to make the riches of traditional Chinese culture available to the west includes the practices of chanting and meditation. They also include other Taoist arts such as opening, closing and generally caring for the Taoist shrines at some Taoist Tai Chi sites and observing festivals associated with them. These practices are not empty or formulaic rituals, but physical and spiritual exercises that complement Taoist Tai Chi. As Taoist Tai Chi brings enormous benefits to people in all health conditions, so do chanting, meditation and the other Taoist temple arts. In fact, often the people who have gained the most benefit from participating in the Society and its activities are usually those who do both Taoist Tai Chi and Taoist meditation and chanting. These are not esoteric practices, but physically and spiritually challenging and rewarding activities that re-align the body, relax body and mind, deepen breathing, resonate through the internal organs and energize every part of the body. They are vital for some people for recovering health and so are important components of Taoist Tai Chi health recovery stories.

No book about Taoism with a chapter in it about Taoist Tai Chi would be complete without an account of its founder, Master Moy Lin-Shin (1931-1998). No book about Taoist Tai Chi that retells some of its health recovery stories in *Health Recovery*, the first book about it intended for a general readership (and so distinct from its own self-published instructions guides and manuals intended for its members and practitioners), would be complete without a chapter about Master Moy. Perhaps appropriately it is the longest chapter in *Health Recovery*, though there is much more that could be said. The inclusion of such a chapter was not done out of any sense of merely fulfilling an obligation to his memory, or the desire to indulge in hero-worship, or to write a 'saint's story' (hagiography). Nor is the dedication of *Health Recovery* to his memory just a ritualistic or polite gesture, the done thing. Just as chanting and meditation became natural topics of conversation in the interviews I conducted as the basis for this book so did the question, 'did you ever meet Mr Moy?'

My aim in asking the question was to gain, and gather together, some impressions about him, to gauge the effect he had on other's lives even if they had not met him, and to preserve both, not only for posterity but also for the present. The aim was not to research a biography, or even to collect anecdotes about him, though there are quite a few of them in *Health Recovery*. Again, these are only the tip of an iceberg. These have now passed into, and are passed on in, the Society as what one member calls 'Mr Moyisms.' 'Mr Moy said this,' 'Mr Moy said that.' There is definitely a desire here to respect his memory, to express gratitude for the gifts he gave and to pass on his oral teaching, especially to those who never met him, but there is also a danger in invoking his name simply as an authority to arbitrate debates. He certainly taught, and expected, obedience and respect, but he also taught principles and virtues, and expected enterprise and initiative. Finding the balance here is a lifelong task. He disliked people waiting for him to tell them what to do. And there is plenty of that to be going on with in following the aims and objectives of the Society.

My aim in asking the question 'did you ever meet Mr Moy?' was, and in including the chapter is, to acknowledge his role in founding the Taoist Tai Chi Society and in teaching Taoist Tai Chi and passing on its health benefits, to allow others the opportunity to express their gratitude and respect for his having done so (as the dedication does on my part too), to record their experience of meeting him (or not) and the impression he made on them, and so to tell their story about the part he played explicitly or implicitly in their health recovery story. He has already figured as a leading actor in many of the health recovery stories already presented in *Health Recovery*. In the chapter of the book devoted to him he figures not so much as an instructor of Taoist Tai Chi, of how to do a move or as a source of techniques, but as a teacher of Taoism, of how to be more compassionate, how to look after other people, how to be a better person, to be more centred, but less self-centred. These lessons are probably harder to learn than those about how to do a move or perform a sequence.

Although chapter 8 of *Health Recovery* focuses on Master Moy, it is not a biography. I think he would be appalled if anyone were to write a biography of him, though there is certainly plenty of material out there besides the anecdotes about him that circulate in the Society and the brief biography of him on the Society website in the page headed 'Our Founder.' His older sister, Mrs Lee, is in her 80s and lives in New York. She has many interesting stories to tell about him and I heard some of them when she visited the Orangeville centre to pay her annual respects to her brother whose ashes are interred in the Columbarium there. If I had wanted to write a biography of him, I would have interviewed her. It would go against a basic Taoist virtue of egolessness though. He certainly was a very remarkable man (as this chapter of *Health Recovery* testifies, if not all the preceding ones of *Health Recovery* testify), but he was a self-effacing, yet strong-willed, person who lived an austere, yet rich, and rewarding life. He was multifaceted and paradoxical, yet simple, and so on. His vision and legacy are amazing.

The Taoist Tai Chi Society is a truly remarkable organization. Run largely by volunteers, it is currently active in 28 countries around the world and is reputedly the largest not-for-profit Tai Chi organization in the world. When Master Moy developed Taoist Tai Chi, he did not just teach Tai Chi — he also founded the Taoist Tai Chi Society. He created a body of people in which Taoist Tai Chi, as well as Taoism, is nurtured, taught and learnt. Thus the Society is a community of Taoist bio-spiritual cultivation and practice. Previously and primarily Taoism was a monastic tradition. Master Moy helped to bring this ancient sacred tradition into the modern secular world. Taoist Tai Chi is taught within the context of the Society and practitioners of Taoist Tai Chi are first and foremost members of the Society. Their allegiance and affiliation is to a Master and a Society, rather than to a 'style' of Tai Chi or to a Tai Chi 'club.' In addition to local branches, Master Moy founded the International Taoist Tai Chi Society Health Recovery Centre at Orangeville outside of Toronto. As the name suggests, this Centre is a focus for Taoist Tai Chi and the Society around the world. As David Kroh says, 'Orangeville is it.' It is a kind of Mecca to which many members of the Society aspire to travel to.

The Society has four aims and objectives. Besides focussing on making Taoist Tai Chi available to all, and promoting its health-improving qualities and cultural exchange, the fourth and final aim and objective of the Taoist Tai Chi Society is:

> to help others: the foundation of Taoist Tai Ch is compassion. Our underlying charitable orientation is in keeping with the Taoist virtues of selflessness and service to others. Our inspiration is the example set by our founder, Master Moy Lin-Shin, who dedicated his life to helping others without seeking personal gain. For this reason all our instructors are volunteers, and all our branches operate on a non-profit basis. We also perform other services within the community, and assist other charities.

The virtue of compassion underpins the teaching of Taoist Tai Chi and the other activities of the Society. The voluntary nature of the Society and the dedication of instructors are topics that came up time and again in the interviews. Everyone has a place to fill and a role a play; everyone is valued for what they can and do give.

6. SACRED SUTRAS

Sutras are the primary sacred texts for Taoists. They can be read and studied in quiet contemplation or chanted alone or with others. Chanting is a vital and integral part and activity of Fung Loy Kok Taoist Tai Chi. Chanting sutras is a physical activity, especially when performed kneeling. The kneeling posture enables the spine to straighten, the diaphragm to relax, the airways and knees to open and for internal energy, or *chi*, to be produced and to circulate through the body. Chanting sutras is also a physical activity as the various sounds emitted at different frequencies resonate inside the body and work on different organs. Chanting or reading sutras is also a spiritual activity as they focus the mind and enable meditation on right and wrong ways of thinking, being and doing.

Laozi's 'Sutra of Inspiration' is 'considered to be one of the fundamental texts of Taoist scripture' (FLK, 2008, p.87). Two Taoist monks from the White Cloud Temple in Beijing and Eternal Spring Temple in Wuhan in China 'named this text as an appropriate text to introduce people to Taoism' (FLK, 2008, p.87). The FLK Institute of Taoism further introduces this sutra:

> In Taoism "inspiration" has a connotation of "resonance." We are "inspired" when we are in "resonance" with heaven. The aim of the sutra is to help us to be "in tune" with our Original Nature of goodness, which is a gift from heaven. (FLK, 2008, p.87)

The Sutra involves 'accumulating good works' and repudiating 'evil deeds' (FLK, 2008, pp.89 and 90). Some of these have definite environmental overtones in line with current thinking about plants and animals, such as 'do not hurt trees, grass, and insects. Be empathetic to the suffering of others. Delight in the joys of others. Help people in desperate need. Save people from harm' (FLK, 2008, p.89). Posters around Melbourne, Australia mounted by animal liberationists are based on the same idea of non-human animals as sentient beings and invite the same response of empathy with their suffering. Evil deeds in this Sutra include 'shooting animals that fly and run. Frightening worms and animals that crawl. Filling in burrows and turning over nests. Injuring young animals and breaking eggs' (FLK, 2008, p.91). This Taoist view of animals contrasts with the Biblical interdiction that 'every swarming creature is an abomination' (*Leviticus* 11: 41), an instance of Biblical ecological folly (see Giblett 2018, pp.14 and 53). Other 'evil deeds' include 'burying insects. Hating. Using chemicals to kill trees' and 'swearing at the wind and rain' (FLK, 2008, p.93). These deeds are evil as they go 'against the harmony and flow of things' (FLK, 2008, p.93), against, in other words, the Tao.

'Not feeling gratitude when helped by others' is another in a long list of 'evil deeds' enumerated in this sutra (FLK, 2008, p.91). Filial gratitude to one's parents in particular, and to Heaven and Earth in general, is specifically enjoined by 'Guanyin's Sutra of Filial Gratitude.' The FLK Institute of Taoism relates how 'Master Moy selected the section of this sutra entitled 'Confession of Gratitude by Son and Daughter' for discussion because the segment contains the gist of the main ideas expressed in the entire sutra' (FLK, 2008, p.31). This sutra for the FLK Institute of Taoism is 'an important sutra' as it 'contains instructions on Taoist training encoded in multiple levels' (FLK, 2008, p.31). In their commentary on this segment of the sutra, the FLK Institute of Taoism explain that two of those levels are that 'Heaven and Earth are the father and mother of all things. Father and mother are also the Heaven and Earth of our body' (FLK, 2008, p.33). Both levels of our blood parents and Heaven and Earth and all four beings make up 'the Tao (the Source)' and 'the whole (the Tao)' (FLK, 2008, p.50). Birth is separation from our parents and from Heaven and Earth. The FLK Institute of Taoism also comments that 'symbolically, the practice of filial gratitude and filial piety is the path of Returning to the Source' by being 'grateful for the Tao's gift of life to us' (FLK, 2008, p.51). Separation also entails separation of our organs into separate units instead of functioning as 'a holistic body' so 'Returning to the Source' involves getting 'our internal organs and every part of our body to function as a connected whole' (FLK, 2008, p.51).

Tai chi exemplifies the training in developing a body that functions as a connected whole. Tai chi is a practice of 'Taoist internal alchemy' in which 'the body is the vehicle for the Return to the Tao' (FLK, 2008, p.52). The Taoist body oriented to the past source of life and living mindfully in the present moment contrasts with the Fascist body in which the body is the vehicle for projection into, and colonisation of, the future (see Giblett, 2008a, chapter 6). The Fascist body of the machine with a hard, metallic surface also contrasts with the Taoist body of the earth with soft, organic depths. The Fascist body aspires to immutability, impenetrability and impermeability, whereas the Taoist body inspires to openness, softness and the flowing quality of water. For the Taoist, 'we must change our bodies' by using 'techniques of changing the tendons' in which 'the spinal column achieves elasticity and openness' (FLK, 2008, p.52). Incorporating the 'Five and Eight Animals,' the five animal forms and the eight animal appearances, into the body is the means for doing so (see chapter 1 of the present volume). 'The body' for the Taoists is 'that which conceives, nourishes, shelters, and gives birth to the Spirit God' (FLK, 2008, p.53). The body for the Fascists is that which conceives, nourishes, shelters, and gives birth to the Machine God.

One of the Taoists favorite sutras for chanting and one of the most frequently chanted is *Goo Yam Gau Foo Ging,* or *The Sutra of Goon Yam who Saves People from Suffering. Goon Yam* is also known as *Guan Yin,* the Bodhisattva of compassion (see chapter 1 of this volume). The second and third lines of this sutra highlight the polytheistic nature of Taoism and Buddhism when they hail 'Buddhas of incalculable number!/Buddhas as numerous as the grains of sand in the River Ganges!' (FLK 2012a, p.3). Compassion is a virtue central to Taoism and Buddhism. *Daai Bei Jau* (FLK 2012a, p.11) is translated as 'Mantra of great compassion.' The fourth aim and objective of Fung Loy Kok Taoist Tai Chi emphasizes compassion as the central underpinning of all its other aims and objectives, and of all endeavors and activities. Guan Yin is the embodiment and expression of compassion, and of wisdom. *The Heart Sutra of the Perfection of Wisdom* addresses and invokes 'the Boddhisattva Guanyin,/Practising deep Perfection of Wisdom' (FLK 2012b, p.8).

The body is central to Taoism; the heart is central to the Taoist body and 'taming the heart' is central to the path of triple cultivation of bodily, spiritual and environmental health. 'Immortal Lü's Sutra of Taming the Heart' (FLK 2008, pp.101-104) is central to Taoism as Immortal Lü is the representative 'deity' of Taoism (representing wisdom) to place alongside the Jade Emperor from Confucianism (representing virtue) and Guan Yin from Buddhism (representing compassion) in the 'three religions' tradition of Fung Loy Kok Taoist Tai Chi (as discussed in chapter 1 of the present volume). The second chant of the *Ten Thousand Buddhas Sutra*, 'Sacred Chant of the Dedication of the Incense,' begins by declaring that 'the Tao is approached through the heart./ Like the smoke of the incense, let the heart rise to the Tao' (FLK 2012c, p.5).

'Taming the heart' means purifying the mind and the mouth. The third and fourth sacred chants of the *Ten Thousand Buddhas Sutra* are devoted to the purification of the mind and the mouth, the gateways to the body and the belly:

> May the pearl of the spirit of speech/Expel the impure air from within us. […]
>
> So that our health is enhanced and our spirit is cultivated. (FLK 2012c, p.7)

This is in line with current medical research that lung compliance (the ability to access and use more of our lungs) is a, if not the, key determinant in longevity (Ryan, *et al*, 1999). Practitioners of Taoist Tai Chi who have had their lung compliance tested report levels of lung compliance above average for their age and commensurate with those of a much younger age group. Anecdotally they also report increased chest size and deeper breathing from regular chanting of sutras and from diligent practice of the other Taoist internal arts of health. As the chant says, 'Everything opens up and connects' inside and outside the body, the inside and the outside connecting with each other. The chant concludes, 'Let the Breath of the Tao forever stay with us' (FLK 2012c, pp.6 and 7). Chanting enables the breath of the Tao to stay forever with us.

The fifth sacred chant of the *Ten Thousand Buddhas Sutra* is devoted to the purification of the body:

> May the Heavenly Venerable One of the Precious Spirit
>
> Protect the form of our being.
>
> Protect the souls of all sentient beings.
>
> Let our internal organs be healthy and strong.
>
> May the Green Dragon and the White Tiger
>
> Guard the innermost depths of our spirit.
>
> May the Raven and Warrior Stars
>
> Protect and strengthen our bodies. (FLK 2012c, p.9)

Practitioners of Taoist Tai Chi who have had bone-density tests before and after taking up the practice of this weight-bearing art of health report increased bone-density. In medical research the jury is still out on whether tai chi in general increases bone density. Part of the inconclusiveness in their findings to date is due to the number of different 'styles' of tai chi and the different emphases they have. Some schools trumpet tai chi as an exercise or art that increases bone density and market themselves to potential and real sufferers of osteoporosis. Taoist Tai Chi is not a specific 'cure' or treatment for specific conditions; it is a holistic art of bodily, mental and spiritual health that recovers and/or maintains functionality and well-being.

The Green Dragon and White Tiger are collections of constellations and sections of the night sky in Chinese astronomy; the Raven and Warrior Stars are constellations. The heavens above are connected to the earth and the body below. Of the four animal forms, the dragon represents the spine and the tiger represents power and strength. They are appropriate animal forms to invoke for protecting and strengthening our bodies, and so reducing the likelihood of breaking bones as we age and our bones become brittle. Tai chi also improves balance and diminishes the fear of falling so reducing the likelihood of falls in the first place. This is in line with current medical research, especially the famous 'FICSIT' study (Wolf, *et al*, 1996). Anecdotal evidence from practitioners of Taoist Tai Chi reports improved balance and reduced fear of falling.

The sixth sacred chant of the *Ten Thousand Buddhas Sutra* is devoted to the purification of Heaven and Earth:

> When Heaven and Earth follow the Natural Way
>
> Impure chi is dispersed. [...]
>
> May the powerful gods of the eight directions
>
> Lead us to follow the natural course. (FLK 2012c, p.9)

The eight directions are the four compass points, plus the four intermediate ones, southeast, southwest, northeast and northwest.

The natural course connects inside and outside:

> Chant this once
>
> And [...] our internal domain will be guarded
>
> The forces of destruction will be dissipated,
>
> And the Breath of the Tao shall forever remain. (FLK 2012c, p.11)

Tai chi is sometimes called 'a martial art for the defense of the inner world' (see chapter 2 of the present volume). Chanting is a material and spiritual art for doing so too.

The seventh sacred chant of the *Ten Thousand Buddhas Sutra* is the 'Sacred Chant of Golden Light' (FLK 2012c, p.11):

> The mysterious source of Heaven and Earth
>
> Is the root of the chi of all things [...]
>
> The source is Golden Light
>
> Permeating everywhere.

It cannot be seen,

It cannot be heard. (FLK 2012c, pp.11, 13)

The Golden Light is another name for the Tao as it cannot be seen and cannot be heard according to chapter 14 of the *Tao Te Ching*.

The 'Sacred Chant of Golden Light' goes on to state that:

It encompasses Heaven and Earth,

And is the source of life for all sentient beings.

Chant this once

And the body will glow with light. (FLK 2012c, p.13)

The enlightened body is the Taoist way; the Taoist body is enlightened. This contrasts with the modern western Enlightenment in which the mind is enlightened and the 'other' is 'endarkened,' whether it be the 'dark continent' of Africa and its people who are denigrated (literally 'blackened'), or the 'dark continent' of female sexuality for modern European male minds, or the black waters of wetlands and their monsters, or the monstrous 'grotesque lower body.' Western enlightenment depends upon and is made possible by 'endarkenment,' whereas Taoist enlightenment transforms body and mind, spirit and earth. The Taoist body glows with a living aura that shines out from within. The modern western technologies of mechanical reproduction shrivel aura to the point that the body becomes a reflective surface for light captured by the lens culminating in the self-regarding and self-reinforcing narcissism of the 'selfie.'

Studying and chanting the sutras mentioned above is an integrated path for the triple cultivation of a healthy body, mind/spirit and environment that complements other Taoist internal arts of health, such as meditation and Tai Chi. The moving meditation of Tai Chi, the still meditation of quiet sitting, the chanting and observing of the sutras and looking after the earth and its plants and animals are an integral way of cultivating the body, mind, spirit and environment for health. Studying and chanting sutras might seem like an esoteric, spiritual practice, but the virtues they avow and the resonances they produce lead to cultivating bodily health that connect to cultivating environ-mental health too. Taoism is truly a path of triple cultivation.

REFERENCES

Allan, S. (1997). *The way of water and sprouts of virtue.* Albany, NY: State University of New York Press.

Ames, R. (1984). The meaning of body in classical Chinese thought. *International Philosophical Quarterly, 24,* 1, 71-53.

Ames, R. (1986). Taoism and the nature of nature. *Environmental ethics, 8,* 317-350.

Barkan, L. (1975). *Nature's work of art: The human body as image of the world.* New Haven: Yale University Press.

Bodde, D. (1991). *Chinese thought, society, and science: The intellectual and social background of science and technology in pre-modern China.* Honolulu: University of Hawaii Press.

Breuer, J. and S. Freud (1893/2004). *Studies in hysteria.* N. Luckhurst (trans.) London: Penguin.

Certeau, M. de (1992). *The mystic fable,* volume one: *the sixteenth and seventeenth centuries,* M. Smith, (trans.) Chicago: University of Chicago Press.

Cheng, C-y. (1986) On the environmental ethics of the *tao* and the *ch'i. Environmental Ethics, 8,* 4 351-370.

Cheng, F. (1994). *Empty and full: The language of Chinese painting.* Boston: Shambhala.

Clark, K. (1939). *Leonardo da Vinci.* rept. London: Penguin.

Daoren. H. (1994). *Back to beginnings.* T. Cleary (trans.). Boston: Shambhala.

Elvin, M. (1989). Tales of *Shen* and *Xin*: Body-person and heart-mind in China during the last 150 years. In M. Feher (ed.), *Fragments for a history of the human body,* Part Two. New York: Zone (pp.266-349).

Farquhar, J. (1994). Multiplicity, point of view and responsibility in traditional Chinese healing. In A. Zito and T. Barlow (eds), *Body, subject and power in China* (pp.78-101). Chicago: Chicago University Press.

Foucault, M. (1981). *The history of sexuality, Volume one: An introduction.* R. Hurley (trans.). (Harmondsworth: Penguin.

Frank, A. (1990). Bringing bodies back in: A decade review. *Theory, Culture and Society 7,* 131-162.

Fulder, S. (1990). *The Tao of medicine.* Rochester, Vermont: Healing Arts Press.

Fung Loy Kok Institute of Taoism. 2008. *A Path of Dual Cultivation: Teachings of the Fung Loy Kok Institute of Taoism.* Toronto: Fung Loy Kok Institute of Taoism.

Fung Loy Kok Institute of Taoism. 2012a. *Goon Yam Gau Foo Ging* [and] *Daai Bei Jau.* Fung Loy Kok Institute of Taoism, trans. Toronto: Fung Loy Kok Institute of Taoism.

Fung Loy Kok Institute of Taoism. 2012b. *The Great Learning*[,] *The Heart Sutra of the Perfection of Wisdom* [and] *the Scripture of Clarity and Stillness.* Fung Loy Kok Institute of Taoism, trans. Toronto: Fung Loy Kok Institute of Taoism.

Fung Loy Kok Institute of Taoism. 2012c. *Ten Thousand Buddhas Sutra.* Fung Loy Kok Institute of Taoism, trans. Toronto: Fung Loy Kok Institute of Taoism.

Giblett, R. (1996). *Postmodern wetlands: Culture, history, ecology.* Edinburgh: Edinburgh

University Press.
Giblett, R. (2006). *Forrestdale: People and place*. Bassendean: Access Press.
Giblett, R. (2007). Black and White Water. In Emily Potter, Alison Mackinnon, Stephen McKenzie and Jennifer McKay (eds) *Fresh water: New Perspectives on Water in Australia* (Melbourne University Press, pp.31-43.
Giblett, R. (2008a). *The body of nature and culture*. Houndmills: Palgrave Macmillan.
Giblett, R. (2008b). *Health Recovery: The* Taoist Tai Chi™ *Way*. London: Shepheard Walwyn.
Giblett, R. (2008c). *Sublime communication technologies*. Houndmills: Palgrave Macmillan.
Giblett, R. (2009). *Landscapes of culture and nature*. Houndmills: Palgrave Macmillan.
Giblett, R. (2011). *People and Places of Nature and Culture*. Bristol: Intellect Books.
Giblett, R. (2018). *Environmental Humanities and Theologies: Ecoculture, Literature and the Bible*. London: Routledge.
Giblett, R and Webb, H. (eds) (1996). *Western Australian Wetlands: The Kimberley and South-West*. Perth: Black Swan Press/Wetlands Conservation Society (Inc.).
Girardot, N., J. Miller and L. Xiaogan (2001). Introduction. In their (eds) *Daoism and ecology: Ways within a cosmic landscape* (pp.xxxvii-lxiv). Cambridge, Massachusetts: Harvard Divinity School, Center for the Study of World Religions.
Graham, A. (1989). *Disputers of the Tao: Philosophical argument in ancient China*. La Salle, Illinois: Open Court.
Hammer, L. (1990). *Dragon rises, red bird flies: Psychology and Chinese medicine*. Barryton, NY: Station Hill Press.
Hay, J. (1983). The human body as a microcosmic source of macrocosmic values in calligraphy. In S. Bush and C. Murck (eds) *Theories of the Arts in China*, (pp.74-102). Princeton: Princeton University Press.
Hay, J. (1994). The body invisible in Chinese art? In A. Zito and T. Barlow (eds), *Body, subject and power in China* (pp. 42-77). Chicago: Chicago University Press.
Henderson, J. (1984). *The development and decline of Chinese cosmology*. New York: Columbia University Press.
Howard, A. (1940). *An agricultural testament*. London: Oxford University Press.
Howard, A. (1947/1972). *The soil and health: A study of organic agriculture*. New York: Schocken.
I-Ming, L. (1988). *Awakening to the Tao*. T. Cleary, (trans.). Boston: Shambhala.
Jefferies, R. (1885/2001). *At home on the earth: A new selection of the later writings*. J. Hooker (ed.). Totnes: Green Books.
Kaptchuk, T. (1983). *Chinese medicine: The web that has no weaver*. London: Rider.
Kirkland, R. (2004). *Taoism: The enduring tradition*. New York: Routledge.
Kleinman, A. (1988). *The illness narratives: Suffering, healing, and the human condition*. New York: Basic Books.
Kohn, L. (1991). Taoist visions of the body. *Journal of Chinese philosophy 18*, 227-252.
Kohn, L. (1992). *Early Chinese mysticism: Philosophy and soteriology in the Taoist tradition*.

Princeton: Princeton University Press.

Kravitz, E. (1998). Physiology of the Tao. Public Lecture Thursday 30th April 1998, Taoist Tai Chi Society of Australia, Fremantle, Western Australia.

Kristeva, J. (1992). *The Samurai: A novel.* B. Bray (trans.). New York: Columbia University Press.

Kuriyama, S. (1994). The imagination of winds and the development of the Chinese conception of the body. In A. Zito and T. Barlow (eds), *Body, subject and power in China* (pp.23-41). Chicago: Chicago University Press.

Kuriyama, S. (1999). *The expressiveness of the body and the divergence of Greek and Chinese medicine.* New York: Zone Books.

Lao Tzu (2001). *Tao te ching: The definitive edition,* J. Star (trans.). New York: Tarcher.

Leopold, A. (1935/1991). Land pathology [1935]. In S. Flader and J. Baird Callicott (eds), *The River of the Mother of God: And Other Essays* (pp.212-217). Madison: University of Wisconsin Press.

Leopold, A. (1949). The land ethic. In *A Sand County Almanac: And Sketches here and there,* (pp.201-226). New York: Oxford University Press.

Leopold, A. (1999). *For the health of the land: Previously unpublished essays and other writings.* J. Baird Callicott and E. Freyfogle (eds). Washington, D.C.: Island Press/Covelo, California: Shearwater Books.

Lévi, J. (1989). The body: The Daoists' coat of arms. In M. Feher (ed.), *Fragments for a history of the human body.* Part One, (pp.105-126). New York: Zone.

Lieh-tzu (1960). *The Book of Lieh-tzu: A Classic of Tao.* A. Graham (trans.). New York: Columbia University Press.

Lloyd, G. and N. Sivin (2002). *The way and the word: Science and medicine in early China and Greece.* New Haven: Yale University Press.

Lukacs, G. (1971). *History and class consciousness: Studies in Marxist dialectics.* R. Livingstone (trans.) London: Merlin Press.

Mauss, M. (1992). Techniques of the body. In J. Crary and S. Kwonker (eds) *Incorporations* (pp.455-477). New York: Zone.

Mitchell, E. (1946). *Soil and civilization.* Sydney: Angus and Robertson.

Needham, J. (1970). *Clerks and craftsmen in China and the West: Lectures and addresses on the history of science and technology.* Cambridge: Cambridge University Press.

Needham, J. (1983). *Science and civilisation in China, Vol. 5, Chemical and chemical technology, Part V, Spagyrical discovery and invention: Physiological Alchemy.* Cambridge: Cambridge University Press.

Netter, F. (1969). Twenty-somite stage (3.2mm) approximately 25 days. In his *The Ciba collection of medical illustrations,* Vol. 5, *Heart* (p.118). West Caldwell: Ciba.

Ni, H-C. (1995). *Hua Hu Ching: The later teachings of Lao Tzu.* Boston: Shambhala.

Pick, J. (1944). *Australia's dying heart: Soil erosion and station management in the inland.* Second revised edition. Carlton: Melbourne University Press.

Po-Tuan, C. (1986). *The inner teachings of Taoism.* T. Cleary, (trans.). Boston: Shambhala.

Po-Tuan, C. (1987). *Understanding reality: A Taoist alchemical classic.* T. Cleary, (trans.).

Honolulu: University of Hawaii Press.

Porter, R. (1997). *The greatest benefit to mankind: A medical history of humanity.* New York: W. W. Norton.

Robinet, I. (1993). *Taoist meditation: The Mao-Shan tradition of great purity,* J. Pas and N. Girardot, (trans.) Albany, NY: State University of New York Press.

Rossbach, S. (1984). *Feng Shui: Ancient Chinese wisdom of arranging a harmonious living environment.* London: Rider.

Ryan, Gerard, Knuiman, Matthew W, Divitini, Mark L., James, Alan, Musk, A. W., Bartholomew, Helen C. (1999). Decline in lung function and mortality: The Busselton Health Study, *Journal of Epidemiology and Community Health* 53: pp.230–234. Also available online at: https://www.ncbi.nlm.nih.gov/pmc/articles/PMC1756854/pdf/v053p00230.pdf

Schipper, K. (1978). Taoist body. *History of Religions, 17,* 355-386.

Schipper, K. (1993). *The Taoist body.* K. Duval (trans.). Berkeley: University of California Press.

Sivin, N. (1974). Foreword. In M. Porkert, *The theoretical foundations of Chinese medicine: Systems of correspondence* (pp.xi-xvi). Cambridge, Massachusetts: The MIT Press.

Skinner, S. (1989). *The Living Earth Manual of Feng-Shui: Chinese Geomancy.* London: Penguin.

Stibbe, A. (1996). The metaphorical construction of illness in Chinese culture. *Journal of Asian-Pacific Communication 7* (3 &4), 177-188.

Sullivan, M. (1962). *The birth of landscape painting in China.* London: Routledge and Kegan Paul.

Tillyard, E. (1943). *The Elizabethan world picture.* Harmondsworth: Penguin.

Turner, B. (1994). Theoretical developments in the sociology of the body. *Australian Cultural History, 13,* 13-30.

Vinci, L. da (1977). *Selections from the notebooks.* I. Richter (ed.) Oxford: Oxford University Press.

Watts, A. (1953). Asian psychology and modern psychiatry. *American Journal of Psychoanalysis, XIII,* 25-30.

Watts, A. (1970). The world is your body. In R. Disch (ed.), *The ecological conscience: Values for survival* (pp.181-193). Englewod Cliffs, N. J.: Prentice-Hall.

Wei-Ming, T. (1989). The continuity of being: Chinese visions of nature. In J. Callicott and R. Ames (eds), *Nature in Asian traditions of thought: Essays in environmental philosophy,* (pp.67-78). Albany, NY: State University of New York Press.

Wolf, S. L., Barnhart, H. X., Kutner, N. G., McNeely, E., Coogler, C., Xu, T (1996). Reducing frailty and falls in older persons: an investigation of Tai Chi and computerized balance training. Atlanta FICSIT Group. Frailty and Injuries: Cooperative Studies of Intervention Techniques, *Journal of the American Geriatric Society,* 44 (5), pp.489-497. Also available online at: https://www.ncbi.nlm.nih. gov/pubmed/8617895

Wong, E. (1987). *The picture of internals*. Toronto: Fung Loy Kok Taoist Temple.

Wong, E. (1996). *Feng-shui: The ancient wisdom of harmonious living for modern times*. Boston: Shambhala.

Wong, E. (2000) (trans.) *The Tao of health, longevity, and immortality: The teachings of immortals Chung and Lü*. Boston: Shambhala.

Wong, E. (2001). *Tales of the Taoist immortals*. Boston: Shambhala.

Zito, A. (1994). Silk and skin: Significant boundaries. In her and T. Barlow (eds) *Body, subject and power in China* (pp.103-130). Chicago: University of Chicago Press.

www.ingramcontent.com/pod-product-compliance
Lightning Source LLC
Chambersburg PA
CBHW072050160426
43197CB00014B/2700